Alan F. Griffin on Reflective Teaching

A PHILOSOPHICAL APPROACH TO THE SUBJECT-MATTER PREPARATION OF TEACHERS OF HISTORY

BY ALAN F. GRIFFIN

NATIONAL COUNCIL FOR THE SOCIAL STUDIES

National Council for the Social Studies

Editorial staff on this publication: Salvatore J. Natoli, Pamela D. Hollar, M. Angela Olson
Design: Dan Kaufman

Library of Congress Catalog Card Number: 92-82721
ISBN 0-8403-8147-6

Copyright © 1992 by National Council for the Social Studies
3501 Newark Street, NW • Washington, DC 20016-3167

Printed in the United States of America
10 9 8 7 6 5 4 3 2 1

Table of Contents

I. Introduction

II. Dissertation

A Philosophical Approach to the Subject-Matter Preparation of Teachers of History:

A Dissertation by Alan F. Griffin

CONTENTS

III. Index 75

Alan F. Griffin:
The Consummate Reflective Thinker and Teacher

Peter H. Martorella
Professor of Social Studies Education
North Carolina State University
Raleigh, North Carolina

It is a delight to introduce Alan Griffin's heretofore unpublished dissertation and assist in making it available to a wider audience of educators than ever before. Griffin (1907–1964) was a true iconoclast among social studies educators. Once described as "a short, stout, cheerful Santa Claus of a man" (Mayer 1961, 380), he managed to leave a rich and vibrant professional legacy although he published little, eschewed involvement in national professional organizations, and generally resisted attempts to proselytize or publicize and promote his views. He also was indifferent to or contemptuous of most of the rubrics leading to professional upward mobility, and violated many of the canons currently associated with effective teaching.

This brief essay and the one that follows by Shirley Engle view Griffin's contributions to the field of social studies education from two different perspectives. Mine is that of a student who knew him over a span of approximately six years at The Ohio State University where he spent his entire career in higher education. During that period, I took a number of courses and seminars with him (at least five that I can recall), and he served as my advisor for three degrees. He also was the university supervisor during my student teaching experience. Our association spanned the period of Griffin's twilight years and some critical junctures in my professional development.

Shirley Engle's perspective is that of a contemporary who engaged in professional dialog with Griffin and who came to know him at first primarily through his students (Engle 1982). In his essay, Engle assesses Griffin's legacy and the relevancy of his reflective theory of teaching for social studies today.

Since Griffin typically avoided many of the traditional avenues to professional influence, his unpublished dissertation and students became the primary vehicles by which his ideas were disseminated and diffused and his national reputation established. Written a half-century ago, the dissertation has been widely circulated and is used as required reading in social studies classes at institutions across the United States. Among other features, it is a model of how to engage students in reflective thinking in social studies classes (Engle and Ochoa 1988).

The 1942 work, *A Philosophical Approach to the Subject-Matter Preparation of Teachers of History*, is apt testimony to Griffin's exceptional skills as a writer and thinker. Refreshingly lucid and succinct, it is sprinkled with humor, anecdotes, and sarcasm. Stories long have circulated concerning its evolution and defense (e.g., see Farley 1978). To his students, it reads much as Griffin actually spoke, sparking images of his dynamic classes.

Despite its half century of wear, the dissertation seems timeless in its message and vision. It is immediately and pointedly relevant to current issues in teacher education and curriculum planning and speaks eloquently and forcefully to the contemporary debates concerning both the role of history in the curriculum (Bradley Commission on History in Schools 1988; National Commission on Social Studies in the Schools 1989) and the issue of which knowledge is of most value in the social studies (Hirsch 1987; Ravitch and Finn 1987). In fact, 20 years after he completed his dissertation Griffin continued to chide historians at the Annual Meeting of the American Historical Association for not having "done their job"—modeling the reflective method in teaching subject matter. Had they done so, he charged, there would be no need for social studies educators.

Griffin, himself, was an exemplar of the reflective method, as expounded by Dewey. Former students, such as Lawrence Metcalf (1963) and Maurice Hunt (Hunt and Metcalf 1955, 1968), have attested to his skills in using the reflective method in his own classes. Shaver and Berlak (1968) have observed that Griffin also was an inspirational teacher. My own memories of him as a teacher, during his later years immediately after he had returned from an emotionally draining three-year project in India, are vivid and rich. He became an indelible model not only for teaching but also to the sweep of his knowledge and verbal and analytical artistry.

Perhaps more than any other professional, Griffin influenced my views on teaching, teacher education, scholarship and intellectual standards, the nature of subject matter, and the relationship of the social sciences and history to the social studies curriculum. Along with H. Gordon Hullfish and Harold Fawcett, both quite different from him, Griffin also served as a sparkling window to Dewey's ideas that permeated the College of Education at The Ohio State University in the 1950s and early 1960s. Surprisingly, he accomplished all this with a minimum of direction, praise, criticism, or exhortation. His custom rather was to challenge you to think critically about all ideas, especially your own. He assumed you would identify and resolve problems about which you were curious. The rewards from such pursuits, if any, were to be intrinsic.

Griffin was a steadfast believer in Dewey's dictum: "Growth depends upon the presence of difficulty to be overcome by the exercise of intelligence." A student in Griffin's life space needed

to be prepared for the recurring emergence of "difficulty," which appeared in many guises. It sometimes surfaced through the medium of sarcasm, which Griffin used deftly and advocated in teaching. Mayer (1961, 217) has quoted Griffin as noting, "Have you ever known a really great teacher who wasn't at least a little bit sarcastic?" With sarcasm, as with his other commentaries directed at students' work, however, Griffin's goal usually was to skewer vividly for the recipient deficiencies in his or her thinking rather than to wound.

As John Farley (1978, 149), Griffin's biographer, has noted, "Griffin liked to say things with a flair." His classes were a smooth blend of spontaneity and well-rehearsed performances that often were replete with extensive body language and mustache massaging. A favored technique was Socratic dialog. Lectures or discussions usually were centered around one or more problems or issues that Griffin labored to make the class experience. Alternately, they involved extended analytical digressions stimulated by a student question that captured Griffin's fancy. Seldom did he use notes or texts, except to quote items. He had a prodigious memory and an excellent background in the classics. These enabled him to interweave myriad disparate facts into a relevant tapestry, whatever the subject under discussion. In addition, his intellectual prowess alternately dazzled and intimidated graduate and undergraduate students alike.

To be sure, Griffin was selective in his pedagogical interests and how he applied his considerable talents to preparing graduates and undergraduates for their respective professional roles. As I recall, he had limited interest in such "how to" matters as, for example, lesson plan formats, objectives, educational media, and classroom management. In his advisor's role, he volunteered little, though he always was available, patient, and helpful when asked for advice. Graduate students concerned with theses, dissertations, deadlines, and bureaucratic regulations found an alternately indifferent and supportive Griffin. His attention span was short for matters of rules, policies, and administrative trivia, and he often played the role of the sympathetic ally in the war against the bureaucracy.

At the same time, he offered students extraordinary freedom to pursue their intellectual interests, however idiosyncratic they might appear. Undergraduate students especially often found this freedom disconcerting rather than liberating and the intellectual challenges threatening instead of conducive to their growth. While an undergraduate, I was sensitive to the fact that students typically were either strongly drawn to or put off by Griffin, with few in between. There is at least some evidence that in his twilight years this feeling was mutual. Mayer (1961, 380–381) reported the following aside by Griffin:

> Every year, early in the term, I hold a conference with each of the students in my course, and I ask them why they want to teach social studies. Nearly all of them give me the same answer—they want to teach democratic values to adolescents. I say "Good. Now in this area of democratic values, can you think of any ideas or opinions you may hold which you think might be suspect, might not be purely democratic—might be the sort of opinion you wouldn't want to insist that your students hold?" And they all say, No, their hearts are pure, everything they believe in is democratic. So I ask another question. I say, "In other words, what you want to do is indoctrinate your students with your values. Is that right?" On their reaction to that, I decide whether or not I'm going to be interested in them.

Griffin assumed that only a few undergraduates would be able to connect with his ideas. He conceded to Mayer (1961, 381), "I get maybe two or three [students] a year who know what I'm talking about."

In sum, we see in Griffin a unique social studies educator, whose singular work a half century later remains the most important translation of Dewey's ideas and the ideals of democracy to the teaching of social studies. A more comprehensive analysis reveals a complex multifaceted individual whose small but notable collection of pedagogical and social issue publications, community service activities, speeches, and teaching practices embodied the principles of democratic action he espoused and profoundly affected those whom they reached. Perhaps Alan Griffin's greatest legacy is the carefully constructed and solid philosophical scaffolding that undergirds his theory of reflective teaching and the rich treasure of ideals, models, and standards he has bequeathed our profession.

References

Bradley Commission on History in Schools. *Building a History Curriculum: Guidelines for Teaching History in Schools.* Washington, D.C.: Educational Excellence Network, 1988.

Engle, Shirley H. "Alan Griffin (1907–1964)." *Journal of Thought* 17 (1982): 45–54.

Engle, Shirley, and Anna Ochoa. *Education for Democratic Citizenship: Decision Making in the Social Studies.* New York: Teachers College Press, 1988.

Farley, John. *The Life and Times of Alan Griffin: Exemplar of Reflection.* Unpublished dissertation, The Ohio State University, Columbus, Ohio, 1978.

Griffin, Alan F. *A Philosophical Approach to the Subject-Matter Preparation of Teachers of History.* Unpublished dissertation, The Ohio State University, Columbus, Ohio, 1942.

Hirsch, E. D., Jr. *Cultural Literacy: What Every American Needs to Know.* Boston: Houghton Mifflin, 1987.

Hunt, Maurice P., and Lawrence E. Metcalf. *Teaching High School Social Studies: Problems in Reflective Thinking and Social Understanding.* New York: Harper and Row, 1955.

Hunt, Maurice P., and L. E. Metcalf. *Teaching High School Social Studies: Problems in Reflective Thinking and Social Understanding,* 2d ed. New York: Harper and Row, 1968.

Mayer, Martin. *The Schools.* New York: Doubleday, 1961.

Metcalf, Lawrence E. "Research on Teaching the Social Studies." In *Handbook of Research on Teaching,* edited by N. L. Gage. Chicago: Rand McNally, 1963.

National Commission on Social Studies in the Schools. *Charting a Course: Social Studies for the 21st Century.* Washington, D.C.: National Commission on Social Studies in the Schools, 1989.

Ravitch, Diane, and Chester Finn. *What Do Our 17-Year-Olds Know?* New York: Harper and Row, 1987.

Shaver, James P., and Harold Berlak, eds. *Democracy, Pluralism, and the Social Studies.* Boston: Houghton Mifflin, 1968.

The Legacy of Alan F. Griffin

Shirley H. Engle
Professor Emeritus of Education
Indiana University
Bloomington, Indiana

Alan Griffin, 1907–1964, was the leading scholar in the United States in the development of a reflective theory of teaching in the social studies field. Griffin's dissertation, *A Philosophical Approach to the Subject-Matter Preparation of Teachers of History*, completed at Ohio State in 1942 may well be the most clearly thought out statement ever written of the necessary goals of the social studies in a democracy as these relate to the learning process, to the content, and to the teaching methods employed in social studies instruction.

Griffin's ideas were heavily influenced by John Dewey. At Ohio State where he did his graduate work his mentor was Boyd Bode who along with Gordon Hullfish were the brightest stars in a clutch of young Deweyan scholars who gave to Ohio State in the 1940s the reputation of being the western bastion of Deweyism and the Progressive Education Movement. Griffin quickly established himself in this heady company as a Deweyan scholar of consequence.

Griffin did not accept all of the ideas sometimes associated with progressive education. He particularly resisted the meaning given by some progressive educators to "learning by doing," which Griffin associated with immediately useful, but otherwise menial, kinds of learning to the neglect of "learning by reflection," through which he saw more substantial matters being learned. Although Griffin resisted the extremes of the project approach whereby education was to be based on the questions raised by children, at the same time, he accepted social problems as a proper concern of study. He thought it imperative that so-called touchy aspects in our society be opened up for full scrutiny, arguing that this would never be done with evenhandedness if not done in schools. Although he embraced a problem approach, he warned against overdependence on it. He also saw usefulness in the study of disciplines, providing the study was directed to the examination of beliefs and providing the study was done in the reflective rather than in the expository mood.

To Griffin the world presented an open vista, incomplete and ready to be formed in more desirable ways through reflection on its problems in the light of its experience. Likewise, he saw democracy as an open society having reached its present state by reflection on human experience and open to further development by further reflection. He resisted fixed ideas of democracy that could be imparted to children by rote without their intellectual participation in the process. Although Griffin is said to have remembered everything he ever read, he abhorred fixed answers and memorization as an education process. He saw facts not as the ends of education but as the means, in a variety of contexts, for fueling reflective thought about questions the answers to which are uncertain or perplexing.

Neither did Griffin find an affinity with reconstructionism in any of its several versions. Education reformers who come with blueprints in hand of what they saw as desirable futures to be imposed on children were as anathema to Griffin as those who would condition children to an unquestioning acceptance of the present.

Despite his differences with the Progressives, Griffin was very much at home at Ohio State in those rather heady days. By all accounts Griffin was a person of extraordinary wit and intelligence. He was deeply committed to the democratic idea, both in mind and in his daily life. Older by about ten years than most graduate students, already a successful high school teacher, and a considerable Deweyan scholar in his own right, he was regarded at Ohio State more as one of the faculty than one of the students. Griffin's orals were reputed to have been one of the mightiest intellectual duels between a student and his mentor ever staged at Ohio State. At one point in his orals, Griffin was said to have been asked a question he was immediately at a loss to answer. After a painful pause, Bode, his chairman, offered to withdraw the question. Griffin demurred and said he would like to try an answer. On completing the answer, Griffin turned to Bode and asked if his answer was correct. Bode is said to have replied, he did not know, explaining that he raised the question because he wanted to know the answer himself, and he thought Griffin would surely know it.

This was a kind of forerunner of Griffin's selection later to debate the fearsome Arthur Bestor, an American historian famous for his vitriolic attacks on the progressive education movement, a debate which, by the accounts of a somewhat biased audience, Griffin won handily. In any case, immediately after his orals, Griffin was added to the faculty of Ohio State where he remained until his untimely death in 1964.

Prior to finishing his dissertation and while he was a graduate student at Ohio State, Griffin wrote *Freedom: American Style*, published by Henry Holt and Company in 1940 and *What Do You Mean—Be Good?*, published by the School and College Service in Columbus, Ohio in 1941. Other writings included radio scripts for a WOSU radio program. entitled "No Corner on Democracy," and a pamphlet series for the "Town Meeting League." Surprisingly, after his dissertation, Griffin wrote almost nothing on the social studies.

Griffin's influence on the social studies came about through his teaching and his students.

He was renowned at Ohio State as a brilliant and erudite teacher and one who practiced the reflective method that he preached. His classes were themselves exercises in reflective teaching. He encouraged his students to question and doubt their beliefs and the beliefs of others. He encouraged and helped them to discover the factual and philosophical grounds, if any, for holding to these beliefs. He was slow to settle any question finally. His students say that he exhibited enormous patience in helping both bright and those not so bright to master this process, which he saw as the crucial element in democratic education. Griffin was more concerned that students learn to think and to enjoy thinking than that they cover material or possess conventional answers to the usual questions.

Griffin's students spread his ideas. Between 1942 and 1964, hundreds of undergraduates at Ohio State came under his tutelage. Many succumbed to his ideology. In addition, Griffin worked with a goodly number of doctoral students at Ohio State. Among these are Maurice Hunt, late of Fresno State University, Lawrence Metcalf, late of the University of Illinois, Peter Martorella of North Carolina State University, James Barth of Purdue University, Dave Martin of the University of Houston, James Durance of Kent State, and M. Eugene Gilliom of Ohio State. Many of these would become distinguished scholars in their own right.

The writer's introduction to Alan Griffin came about through a contact with some of his students. The writer was teaching at the Pre-School Teachers Institute of the Cincinnati (Ohio) Public Schools in the fall of 1958. A group of young teachers in the class were clearly a cut above the others. They were more seriously committed to the social studies, more questioning, more critical, and generally more intellectually demanding than were the others. Out of curiosity, the writer asked who they were and where they came from. They proudly informed him that they were students of Alan Griffin.

Alan F. Griffin on Reflective Teaching

In preparing to write this introduction, the writer reread Griffin's famous dissertation. It is as fresh and relevant to the problems that beset the social studies today as it was when it was written in 1942. It should be required reading by every student who is preparing to teach the social studies today and it should be required reading by every group, committee, or commission set up to reform the social studies. It should be required reading for anyone who is interested in education for democracy.

A PHILOSOPHICAL APPROACH TO THE SUBJECT-MATTER
PREPARATION OF TEACHERS OF HISTORY

DISSERTATION

Presented in Partial Fulfillment of the Requirements for
the Degree of Doctor of Philosophy in
the Graduate School of The Ohio State University
By
ALAN FRANCIS GRIFFIN, B.S. IN ED.
The Ohio State University
1942

Ohio State University Archives

Alan F. Griffin
1907–1964

CONTENTS

I
ORIGINS OF THE PROBLEM

Among the more distinctive characteristics of the period in which we are living is the tendency, rapidly becoming world-wide, toward impatience with theory, an impatience which even in America, has already begun to crystallize in the conviction, variously expressed, that "theory doesn't get you anywhere." Even from teachers, on whose part a denial of the importance of theory is equivalent to professional and intellectual suicide, comes a demand for "less theory and more implementation", a demand which may at points be warranted, but which ordinarily means no more than that teachers, too, are a part of the world culture which today is seeking surcease through action from the frustrations of thinking and learning.

It is fair to say that the twentieth century brought revolutionary changes in the outlook of teachers. The recognition that many and perhaps most of the activities of our schools were being carried on as a matter of sheer habit, that "procedures were not related to objectives", that examination of what we were doing in the light of what we thought we were trying to do was urgently needed literally swept across the educational world, carrying all before it. Matters which had been settled became doubtful; the exclamation points of our tradition were replaced by question marks; from attics and cellars we rooted out our dusty Q.E.D.'s, and hastily penciled after each one a parenthetical "but is it?"

Meanwhile, life went on. Schools went on, and so did the preparation of teachers. Changes in procedure were obvious everywhere; educators, shaken out of uncritical complacency, began a feverish and fumbling quest for something to do that would not be vulnerable to the many caustic and easily documented denunciations of "traditional" education which, after a brief initial shock, had come to be accepted as clearly justified.

Inasmuch as one way to deal with any problem is simply to dismiss it, we ought not now to be surprised at the considerable number of educators who grew impatient of the huge task that seemed to have opened up, and who adopted as a basis for action, "Enough of theory. Let's get down to business."

At this point began, for many forward-looking teachers, a period, not of high-hearted adventure, but of almost unbearable frustration. Their habitual practices stood revealed as *merely* habitual almost at the instant of stopping to take a look at them. But the justifications for other and different procedures were by no means clear. Teachers were generally willing, so far as they were able, to undertake the education of "the whole child", to try to teach with due regard for physical and mental health, for wholesome and satisfying personal-social relationships, for the needs of young people, for individual differences, for the problems of maturation, for the whole unwieldy body of important considerations that grew up as a purported set of guide-lines to direct teachers toward a more effective practicing of their profession. The confusion lay in the simple question, "What *is* our profession? What is it that we are expected to *do* with due regard for all these important matters?"

Struggling under the bales of mimeographed and printed materials (generally quite sound and potentially useful) which continued to increase the adjectival and adverbial literature of education, teachers cried out for a few nouns and verbs. After all, they were only people, not demi-gods. And it was clear that, if they were to take full responsibility for the total development of all the children with whom they had contact, the teacher's function could not be delimited at all. The length of the working day would be determined, not by a realization that the day's tasks had been discharged, but by the onset of exhaustion or by arbitrary creation of time limits. Any attempt to take time for participation in normal recreational activities would perforce be accompanied by a sense of guilt, whose proportions varied with the teacher's conception of the magnitude and urgency of his professional duties.

Teachers began to realize that the pupil had a home, that the kind of home from which he came had much to do with his development, and that the teacher's responsibility could therefore extend to improving the pupil's home environment, which might mean anything from undertaking the education of his parents to improving or supplementing his diet. Other obvious needs of some pupils—for better clothing, for medical or dental care, for glasses, for parental affection, for membership in a "gang" or "crowd", for an almost unlimited range of material things or of relationships which our culture has, to its shame, been unable to vouchsafe to every boy and girl, provided additional jobs for the school and consequently for the teacher.

In fact, of course, the school did not make itself over into a gigantic social-service agency. The effect of looking at the school as an institution designed to meet all the needs of all the children was not so much to alter the practices of teachers in general as to impress conscientious teachers with an overwhelming sense of frustration, inadequacy, and even down-right guilt.

Only masochists with an evangelical turn of mind could flourish under such a conception of the teacher's function. For, if we once grant that a full statement of the needs of each pupil, plus a list of the qualities a teacher could well cultivate, the matters a teacher might well take into account, and the areas of human knowledge with which the teacher could profitably become conversant constitutes a reasonable basis for determining the teacher's duties, it follows inescapably that no one can teach adequately and that good teachers are merely those whose failure is relatively less complete, or less obvious, than more people's.

Of course, nobody ever intended to place upon teachers—or upon schools, either, for that matter—total responsibility for seeing that every child had everything necessary for optimal development. Perhaps as thorough-going a reliance upon the "needs" concept as may be found anywhere in the literature of education is displayed by the committee[1] which prepared the volume "Science in General Education"; but the committee obviously does not see the science teacher, or even the school, as actually trying to "meet the child's needs" in the social-service sense suggested above. Their view is rather that the "tensions, urges, desires, needs of an individual" are "strategic....in his behavior and its reconstruction."

"These needs not only determine the way in which he sees situations and modifies them, but they also furnish clues to the ways in which it is possible to deal effectively and educationally with him."

This is a long way from suggesting that the teacher's job is to get every pupil's needs "met", or his tensions released, or his urges satisfied. Rather, the needs of pupils are to be capitalized so far as possible in the educative process, and teachers are to take them into account as they deal with individuals. For example, the youngster's "need for increasingly mature relationships in home and family life" is to be met primarily by helping him to achieve relevant insights and "understandings". The authors hasten to point out that "understanding is not offered as a panacea for the adolescent's difficulties in his family relationships."[2] In other words, the claim is not that the child's needs are fully "met" by the process suggested, but rather that the need provides an opportunity for learning and a way in which the teacher can make some aspects of his work vital and significant for the individual student. The pupil's needs do not, apparently, even for those who lean heavily upon them in curriculum construction, determine the direction of a school, or furnish a teacher with ready-made purposes. They provide, insofar as they have been adequately determined, a useful body of data which should be taken into account by teachers. But they neither imply nor effectively substitute for a social ideal.

More than anything else, perhaps, the sensitive teacher needs an answer to the question, "What is my major job, anyway?" Granting, as we must, that absolute limits are impossible, that the teacher's job will always be capable of unlimited extension, and that a wide acquaintance with pre-adolescent and adolescent psychology and a thorough knowledge of the tensions, concerns, and problems of each student would be highly useful to a teacher who knew what he was about, the fact remains that these things do not provide direction. They rather relate to manner than define purpose. "Learning to dance gracefully" is a refinement upon "learning to dance", and we must be clear about the meaning of the latter expression before the former can make much sense to us. In the same way, "teaching history with due regard for a wide variety of social and psychological considerations" can mean very little as a guide either to practice or to judgments of practice until we are fairly clear as to what "teaching history" means. If it turns out to mean nothing useful, clarity on that point will be of great help in making a new start.

To the question, "What do the words 'teaching history' mean?" a variety of answers are possible; but all meaningful answers must be arrived at in one or the other of two fairly well defined ways:

It is possible, in the first place, to examine and analyze the activities of people who assert that they are "teaching history" or about whom others make that assertion. This procedure will give us a meaning for "teaching history" which treats the two words together as a single identifying symbol, without regard for the customary meanings of either one. Used in this sense, the expression "history teaching" has indeed a genuine operational meaning. It points directly to a number of specific behaviors which are conventionally accepted as evidence that "history

teaching" is going on. In the same way, one could identify certain behaviors on the part of a witch-doctor with the label "exorcising a demon", whereupon that phrase would have a clear operational meaning, which could be understood without any reference to what the component words "exorcise" and "demon" might mean in this context. If anyone inquired, "Is that fellow *really* exorcising a demon?" the response, "Of course he is. Can't you see him waving those feathers?" would make perfectly good sense, so long as we considered the phrase only in the way indicated above.

The second approach would be to treat "teaching history" as two separate words, and then to develop a theory purporting to warrant their juxtaposition. In this case, our question is not, "What are the specific activities to which the label 'history teaching' is generally attached?" but rather, "What does the teacher of history *think* he is doing? What state of affairs does he envisage as resulting (at least optatively) from the activities he carries on?"

Obviously an inquiry limited to the first of these questions, "What do those who are said to be 'teaching history' actually do?" would be useful in teacher preparation only insofar as the goal of enabling people to hold down jobs as history teachers was accepted as significant and worth while. The alternative approach, an inquiry into what the teaching of history is expected to accomplish, necessarily involves a task which to some may seem remote from the subject of this study, namely, the development of a theory of the possible roles of historical materials within the learning process. Nevertheless, the writer believes that any thorough-going attempt to secure direction for the subject-matter preparation of history teachers must begin by providing a theoretical basis from which to answer the question, "What is it that the history teacher is being prepared to do?"

Many will say that there is no need to make heavy weather of this question. We are fairly well agreed as to what materials may be spoken of as "history", and the teacher's task is to bring youngsters into contact with those materials. What happens after that is almost wholly unpredictable, but there is ample evidence that many people profit from the contact, and this is enough to justify continuing to maintain social arrangements which guarantee that the contact will take place. "If a man knows history, he knows what it's good for; and if he doesn't know history, nobody can tell him."

That men do read history, study history, conduct historical research, and construct a wide variety of historical syntheses is a matter beyond possible doubt. Because the word "why" is nearly always ambiguous, the question, "Why do men do these things?" is a bifurcated question. That is to say, we may answer it by attempting to set forth the *causes* of men's behaving in these ways, or we may answer it by attempting to determine the consciously held purposes ("reasons") which impel men so to behave. These two answers are in no sense mutually exclusive; it is obvious, for example, that where "motive" can be discovered, it becomes an important aspect of the "causes" (i.e., the explanation) of any line of conduct. On the other hand, the possibility of behavior (even highly complex behavior like historical research) without clear motive or conscious purpose beyond the action itself must not be overlooked.

It is entirely possible for one man to become interested in history as another becomes interested in philately or poetry or contract bridge. That is to say, dealing in one way or another with materials generally called "historical" is one of the possibilities for action which our culture affords, and a dynamic organism may come to elect that kind of action in preference to such other possibilities as it encounters during its search for satisfying stimuli to which to respond. Interaction with historical materials will then become, of itself, a valued kind of behavior, whether it take the form of insatiable reading, or of building a new synthesis, or of tracking to its lair a commonly held misapprehension. This kind of interest in

history may combine with other interests, concerns, and values, and with the accidents of living, to produce such varied manifestations as a Fraser, a Schliemann, a Dennis, a Mommsen, and a Turner.

With history in this sense, as one of the many possibilities for action within our present culture, the professional teacher of history in the secondary school has no particular concern, except as he can capitalize upon an interest of this kind for the purposes of general education. He has the same obligation to nourish and foster this interest as he would have to nourish and foster any other promising interest, and no more. Certainly the development of interest in history as such cannot be a necessary part of his professional function; often he will not share such an interest himself. If significant interest in history as such were made a requirement for certification as a teacher of history, it is possible that some excellent teachers would be eliminated from the profession.

Obviously, there is no reason under the sun for discouraging anyone who finds satisfaction in any of the various activities associated with or related to history from enjoying himself to his heart's content. A case can even be made for providing at public expense opportunities and facilities for this kind of activity. But history as a school subject, and especially as a *required* school subject, cannot take its sanction from any such source.

The present study is concerned with the subject-matter preparation of history teachers. It will not attempt to deal with the question, "Should colleges of education continue to prepare teachers of history?" The writer is fully conscious of the considerable opposition to the teaching of history as a separate subject in secondary schools, and of the perceptible movement toward some sort of core curriculum or its equivalent; and he readily grants that the program of preparation for history teachers ought to equip them to make their contributions within a core curriculum. However, the high probability[3] that history as a separate subject will be taught in most secondary schools for many decades seems adequate warrant for continuing to prepare teachers of history, at least for some time to come.

The present writer has been unable to find anyone who will say flatly, "The subject-matter preparation of history teachers need not be guided by a conception of what history teachers are supposed to do with subject-matter." That there is at least some presumptive connection seems so obvious that one is somewhat diffident about saying it. Yet the casual fashion in which departments of education "farm out" students to subject-matter specialists, and the absence from educational literature of any but the most perfunctory allusions to how teacher-controlled subject-matter is supposed to function within the experience of children, forces the conclusion that few institutions have taken the question seriously.[4]

Students who are preparing to teach in secondary schools are ordinarily required by reputable colleges of education to devote from one-third to two-fifths of their total time[5] in college to so-called "subject-matter" preparation. That colleges of education attach great importance to this activity is attested by (1) the prevalence of special requirements in terms of marks or grades, in the student's "subject-matter areas", (2) the specialized character of typical "methods" courses and (3) the simple fact that student time equivalent to more than a year of full-time residence work must ordinarily be devoted to "subject-matter preparation" in the student's "area of specialization" alone.

Students who have questioned the purposes or the utility of their subject-matter preparation (frequently on the ground that they have forgotten almost all of it by the time they are ready for student teaching) report that they generally receive some such answer as, "After all, it is probably wise for a teacher to know a little something about the materials he is teaching." This truism, undebatable as stated, begs the question students raise when they contend that it is precisely the failure of their subject-matter preparation to result in a reasonable knowledge of materials which causes their concern. A distinguished social scientist reminds us that whenever a belief is so clearly sound that "to inquire into it would be absurd, obviously unnecessary, unprofitable, undesirable, bad form, or wicked, we may know that the opinion is a non-rational one, and probably, therefore, founded upon inadequate evidence."[6]

The idea that people who are going to teach something called "history" ought to prepare for this activity by studying something which is also called "history" is plausible enough on the face of it. But virtually all sympathetic magic has a certain plausibility. Fraser tells us that a soldier of Madagascar dared not eat kidneys, because, the words for "shot" and "kidney" being identical in the Malagasy language, he would surely be shot in battle if he did so.[7] This notion does not compare too unfavorably in plausibility with the view that one who expects to teach algebra and geometry, called in English "mathematics", may profitably struggle with the calculus, also called in English "mathematics". Presumably a case can be made for this latter procedure, but making that case involves the development of a theory purporting to explain exactly how the one activity may enter into and affect the other. The soul-substance theory, for example, could have explained the matter easily, in terms of the greater development of relevant faculties through formal discipline. But that theory has been publicly and overwhelmingly discredited, so that we are compelled either to justify practice by more adequate theory or to take our magic straight.

The idea that the study of college "history" will be useful *per se* to teachers of high school "history" has an especial plausibility because the term "history", at all levels, defies definition. As nearly as the writer can learn, "history" seems to refer, strictly speaking, to "anything that has been found out by what is called 'historical method'." Kepler's laws belong to natural science, because they were fashioned by "scientific method"; but the story of how, in the effort to order and synthesize the data collected by Tycho Brahe, Kepler was led to the hypothesis of the elliptical orbit is a story belonging to history, since its facts are "documented" rather than "proved". Inasmuch as no significant part of the required work in history, either for secondary school students or for their teachers, is ordinarily devoted to a consideration of historical method, it is clear that only the familiarity of tradition and the hesitancy of polite people to raise questions that do violence to the categories of use and wont have enabled the concept "school history" to retain any meaning at all. This question is treated in more detail in the next chapter; for the present, it is enough to point out that the relationship between required subject-matter preparation and the teaching of history is anything but "self-evident", and that a theory of that relationship is a necessary preliminary to gaining intelligent control over the subject-matter preparation of history teachers. Present practices in that area are grounded largely in an anachronistic educational psychology, sheer habit, a kind of faith analogous to homeopathic magic, or at best a trial-and-error empiricism within which the detection of any but the most egregious errors—or successes either—is close to impossible.

It may appear at first that the approach proposed in this study is needlessly difficult, and that a clear statement of objectives, sincerely followed in practice, would adequately serve the needs both of teachers of history in the secondary schools and of those concerned with teacher-preparation. The present writer has no such faith. Sad experience has shown him the weird multiplicity of objectives for every subject in the curriculum that results from a reliance upon goals set up out of relation to a theory comprehensive enough at least to furnish some suggestions as to the probable adequacy of a given curricular hypothesis. No one has better summarized the state of affairs than Ernest Horn,[8]

who, after describing studies which revealed, among other things, 1400 objectives being pursued by teachers of American history, 85 objectives in the introduction to one unit in the social studies, and 47 mimeographed pages of objectives in a single junior high school course of study, proposed as a substitute for "objectives" the introduction of every unit with the biblical injunction:

Finally, brethren, whatsoever things are true, whatsoever things are honest, whatsoever things are pure, whatsoever things are lovely, whatsoever things are of good report; if there be any virtue, and if there be any praise, think on these things.

Horn's forthright statement contrasts oddly with the formulations of other recent writers in the field of social studies methods. Wesley, for example, offers as "suggestive" his own arrangement of Beard's list,[9] which includes nine skills, seven habits, eleven attitudes, eight qualities, and a separate category labeled "information". He goes on to present seventeen objectives of his own for history (thirty-six more are shared by economics, geography, civics, and sociology), which include such familiar phrasings as, "To develop an appreciation of our social heritage," "To acquire a perspective for understanding contemporary issues," "To develop a love of historical reading," "To promote international understanding." He then warns teachers against the danger of trying to "analyze every step in order to state the specific purpose for taking it," because to do so might lead to "the obscuring of the larger and more fundamental objectives," which are stated nowhere in the book, unless, indeed, his own lists are presumed to constitute them. In any case, whatever they may be, "the trend of thinking in the social studies is toward larger objectives." Indeed, "the chief value of studying objectives is the inevitable (heaven knows why!) widening of the teacher's social interests." Oddly enough, "these interests lead in turn into an intensified interest in the psychological powers and social possibilities of pupils." However, Wesley has taken the precaution to point out that, after all, the determination of objectives is carried on by "writers, editors, speakers, public officials, advertisers, legislators, textbook writers, boards of education, committees, pressure groups, and all kinds of organizations." He grants that "the social studies teacher, because of his interest and competence, *should not hesitate to play his part.*" [10]

Another recent methods text covers the problem of objectives in American history as follows:

> The important fact is for the teacher to make his purpose definite so that his teaching can be efficient. In a democratic country, preparation for citizenship should be preparation for actual participation in a free society. This implies learning how to make intelligent choices, for it is only by actual experience that a genuine appreciation of democratic procedure is developed. Critical-mindedness should include knowing the efforts made by pressure groups to establish their points of view and knowing how to determine truth. It should certainly be the purpose of a teacher in a democracy to show that nations, races, and classes are interdependent. The fact that the United States is a product of the mingling of races and cultures gives ample opportunity to make this objective real. Certainly skill in the obtaining and evaluating of information should be a purpose in the teaching of all history. The teaching of American history, furthermore, should stimulate a respect for the opinions and rights of others, and a well-grounded pride in the achievements of individuals, the community, and the nation, as well as a genuine appreciation of the great American traditions and a love for the ideals of those who laid the basis for this country. Finally, no teaching of the social studies can be adequate unless a continuing interest in social thinking and activity is developed. [11]

The present writer is unable to work out a meaning for most of this paragraph; indeed, he sees the third sentence as a palpable *non sequitur.* But what he does understand of it brings no clarity; for example, the difficulties of persuading anyone who had achieved even a modicum of "critical-mindedness" to love the thoroughly disparate ideals of Jefferson, John Adams, Hamilton, and Franklin, to name only a few of those who presumably "laid the basis for this country" are for the present writer quite overwhelming.

The sort of thing illustrated by the foregoing quotations is objectionable on at least three counts (four, if aesthetic considerations are allowed to operate): (1) it provides little or no direction; (2) it inhibits the search for more adequate bases of action by instilling into the gullible an unwarranted sense of security; (3) it fosters and nourishes the habit of engaging in fuzzy and ungrounded verbalizing, which is one of the most serious handicaps now impeding the professionalizing of education.

If anyone were to ask a physician why he administered insulin, he would probably point out that the diabetic's deficiency of the hormones normally produced by the islands of Langerhans required the administration of some substance which would perform the work of converting starches and sugars into forms which the body could utilize. If a mechanic were asked why he had stepped up a generator, he might say, "Because your battery is low, although you just had it recharged a short time ago. Do a lot of night driving, don't you?" Doctors and mechanics work in terms of theories, as do all practical men. A doctor who said, "I am performing this operation in order to facilitate the optimal functioning of the patient's whole being, and thus render him a better citizen, make his home and family life more edifying, enhance his aesthetic appreciations, and enable him to develop worthwhile interests," would often assert no more than the truth, but he would regard the assertion as banal rather than profound. Indeed, it is probable that only the writers of advertising copy, who sell beauty rather than soap, popularity and the amazed approval of one's intimates rather than music lessons, or refreshing pauses rather than carbonated drinks, can appropriately be compared to teachers "stating their purposes."

In the absence of adequate theory, all of us are reduced to the sheer empiricism of the alchemist, mixing together all sorts of accidental combinations "in order to" turn base metal into gold. The formula is, "Decide what outcome you want, then do whatever occurs to you (or, more often, whatever you are accustomed to do), and last of all 'evaluate' by trying to find out whether your desired result has taken place." This approach is certainly not to be condemned out of hand; occasionally it yields remarkable results, and sometimes no other method is available at a moment when action is urgently required. No one will deny that a blind man with a gun can conceivably kill a duck on the wing. The fact remains, however, that alchemy is not science; neither can education be a profession while educators attempt to operate without a clearly formulated theory that explains and directs what they are doing.

The attempt to find or build such a theory will take us over a wide range of territory. In the next chapter, we shall explore the nature of history as a school subject, less in the hope of finding leads there than in the conviction that we ought to know what our theory is about when we get it put together. In chapter three we shall consider certain implications of the democratic ideal for the teaching of history. Chapter four deals with the unique function of information in a democracy. Chapter five attempts to outline a theory of the role of historical materials inside the learning process. Chapter six attempts to draw out enough curricular implications of the theory to indicate its practical direction and to test (so far forth) its validity. In chapter seven we return to the question with which we began: What should be the character of the history teacher's subject-matter preparation?

Perhaps there is a simpler and shorter way to get at this question. Certainly, to raise a question and then to spend six chapters in merely getting ready to deal with it is by no means orthodox procedure. However, Sir John Fraser devoted thirty years to a search for the answer to the single question, "Why had Diana's priest at Nemi to slay his predecessor, after first plucking the bough of a certain tree?" Perhaps the conclusion should be that it takes time to investigate matters which, at least ostensibly, involve a reliance upon magic.

II
THE NATURE OF HISTORY
AS A SCHOOL SUBJECT

Almost everyone, before the latter part of the nineteenth century, would have regarded any inquiry into the nature of history as a work of supererogation. History was what people studied in history courses. The content of these courses was obtained by gathering together enormous quantities of "facts" unearthed by patient scholars, "omitting all their characteristic details, and summarizing them in the most general, and therefore vague, expressions....Nothing was left but a residue of proper names and dates connected by formulae of a uniform type; history appeared as a series of wars, treaties, reforms, revolutions, which only differed in the names of peoples, sovereigns, fields of battle, and in the figures giving the years."[12]

In the words of Henry Johnson,[13] "History was simply one of those words the meaning of which was clear to everybody and only when people began to ask 'What is history?' was it discovered that nobody seemed to know, and that the more they thought about it the less they seemed to know."

The question, "What is history?" has been answered in a variety of ways so wide as to suggest that the question itself has been badly framed. So far as school history courses are concerned, the "what-is-it?" question may be approached by recognizing that their "historical" content will be derived largely from one or more text-books, and then raising the question Beard has posed to his fellow-historiographers, "What do we think we are doing when we write history?"[14]

It is unlikely that most writers of school histories, if they have thought about this question at all, would willingly place themselves in the ranks of those scholars who "are dominated, from monograph to many volumed work, by one clear-cut ideal—that presented to the world first in Germany and later accepted everywhere, the ideal of the effort for objective truth."[15] Nevertheless, an examination of most of the text-books now in use in secondary school courses in world history and American history suggests no other ostensible justification for much of their content. It is true that many text-books profess, in their introductions and occasionally even in an opening chapter, to set forth the principles of selection which have determined their content; these explanations, as one would expect, seldom attempt to be more than superficial.[16] Their stock thesis is that we must know the past in order to understand the present, because the present grew out of the past. The assumption that "the past" will be made available to the student through the history text-book is ordinarily not stated, but always implied. Frequently an author will point out that the facts need to be "organized" under a variety of headings or categories, and that he has included only the "important" facts, or those which are calculated to help in "illuminating the present."

A careful reading of any high school text-book, carried on in terms of the steady question "Why is *this* particular incident or episode included?" rarely produces more than a handful of clear-cut answers, if we eliminate the appeal to "objective truth." Most of the incidents are included, so far as one can tell, just because "that's what actually happened." And many will say, "Reason enough."

One is forced to the view that, while text-book writers intend to give the youngsters the important facts, they are not seriously disturbed by such questions as what "give" in this sense may mean, or how "*the* facts" are selected from an almost limitless mass of factual statements that could be offered, or how "importance" in this connection is determined.

As a matter of realistic practice, the text-book writer is generally held by his editors and publishers, for competitive reasons, to the highly empirical standard, "Any event or person named in most text-books of a given general scope should likewise be named in any new text-books of the same general scope." This limitation, of course, does not bind the text-book writer either to treat the customary "facts" in exactly the usual way or to restrict himself simply to the traditional "facts". He may within limits, interpret matters according to his fancy; and he may include many "extra" facts, if he chooses, so long as he omits none of the conventional ones. Indeed, if several writers chance to include a particular new "fact", the traditional content is expanded and the innovation becomes mandatory upon subsequent writers. Moreover, there is a slow but perceptible dropping out of materials whose right to recognition as "factual" has been clearly and publicly exploded.

About all we can guarantee, then, is that school texts in history will contain a traditionally accepted body of "facts", plus such other facts as the author for any reason deems important, and that in all probability the writer and several other presumably competent persons believe the statements made in the book to be substantially correct.

So far as historiographers are concerned, however, "respect for truth" has meant, in operational terms, a steady reliance upon the integrity and competence of critical scholars and research workers. Langlois'[17] description of the state of affairs at the close of the nineteenth century is perhaps less appropriate than when it was written, but it is by no means out of date:

> The historians....cultivated the species of literature which was then known as "history", without considering themselves bound to keep in touch with the work of the scholars. The latter, for their part, determined by their critical researches the conditions under which history must be

written, but were at no pains to write it themselves. Content to collect, emend, and classify historical documents, they took no interest in history, and understood the past no better than did the mass of their contemporaries.

The ideal of "objective history" which James Harvey Robinson has defined as "history without an object", may properly be invoked by men who are impelled to investigate, simply for the joy of doing so, the warranted assertibility of statements purporting to describe events alleged to have occurred at some past time. The process is highly reflective and often laborious. One cannot fail to respect the amazing erudition of a scholar who can dismiss Herodotus' assertion that the Etruscans came originally from Greece, migrated to Lydia, and thence made their way to Italy, on the ground that such an event as their mass exodus would surely have been known to and reported by the Lydian historian Xanthus. The fact that Xanthus' works are (up to now, at least,) totally lost is no insuperable barrier to the scholar in developing his proof, because Dionysius of Halicarnassus was thoroughly familiar with them, and would certainly not have neglected to report, in his own discussion of the Etruscans, any relevant statements Xanthus might have made![18]

To the question, "So what?" scholars rarely return an answer; it is not, however, their methodology or their painstaking thoroughness which is brought under fire by that indecorous question. With equal care Sidney Fay set out to discover whether the event known as the "Potsdam Conference" (or "Potsdam Council") ever took place. In this case, however, the *belief* that there had been a Potsdam Conference was a part of the attitude of many Americans toward Germany and toward the Versailles treaty. If the conference did take place, as described by Morganthau, Poincare, Lichnowsky, and others, that fact warranted, so far forth, the judgment that Germany's treatment had not been unduly harsh. Fay, frankly a "revisionist", could not reconcile the nefarious "Council" with the absence of evidence that either the German government or German industry had *acted upon* the decisions it was alleged to have reached. Fay's clear proof[19] that the "Potsdam Conference" was a myth did not, indeed, prove that Germany was being unjustly penalized; it *did* prove that one assertion frequently used to justify the Versailles treaty was groundless.

Obviously, Fay was operating from a bias. His bias probably accounts for his selection of one particular statement to investigate, rather than another of the countless assertions about past events that could well be doubted. From the point of view of sheer scholarship and the pleasure of exercising research skills, one could quite as well join the earnest students who have reduced Pinckney's ringing "Millions for defense, but not a cent for tribute," to the colorless, "No, no; not a sixpence," or converted Ethan Allen's majestic demand for surrender "in the name of the great Jehovah and the Continental Congress" into the presumably accurate and thoroughly uninspiring, "Come out of there, you damned old rat."

The question is finally one of how to decide what is worth bothering about. Fay clearly agreed with James Harvey Robinson that the proper use of historical knowledge was to throw light on "the quandaries of our life today." Was he, then, less concerned for "getting the facts" than the scholars who finally demonstrated that William Dawes had in fact played the role assigned by Longfellow to Paul Revere, thereby quite unwittingly demonstrating also how much more effective poetry has been than history in establishing belief? In Beard's words:

> Is the scholar who seeks knowledge useful to his contemporaries wrestling with "the quandaries of our life today" unconcerned about the truth of that knowledge? His end may be different, but surely he does not seek falsehood or believe that false history can be useful to the end posited....As far as method goes, those

scholars who are placed in opposition to the noble dream [of writing history "wie es eigentlich gewesen ist"] may be as patient in their inquiries and as rigorous in their criticism and use of documentation as the old masters of light and leading.[20]

In other words, even research in history is necessarily guided by a frame of reference of some kind. The frame of reference will not, indeed, dictate the research worker's findings, but it will in large measure determine what he is to consider worth investigating. His "objectivity" springs, not from the absence of personal concern or interest in the matter he is investigating (an odd sanction on the face of it, since the tenacious pursuit of a matter to which one is indifferent sounds like a peculiarly complicated sort of *tic*), but rather from the fact that his methods and his materials are deliberately left open for critical examination by others in his field, or by anyone else who cares to take the trouble.

In brief, then, history for the research scholar is the process of inquiring into whether or not certain bits of purported knowledge are sufficiently grounded to warrant calling them "facts". He may carry on this activity either because he is interested in checking the soundness of some of the further conclusions with respect to present day living toward which an alleged "fact" tends; or because he is in love with the activities of a research specialist, enjoying them as other men enjoy swimming, or working cross-word puzzles, or playing chess; or for both reasons. He and his activities rarely get within gunshot of a high school classroom. The reasons for devoting space to him here are two. The first, of course, is to make the point that the research specialist is almost certainly the only sort of person who deals with history *primarily* "in order to find out what the facts are", and even he frequently has other purposes, clear or inchoate.

The second reason for discussing the research historian in this connection is less obvious.

It cannot be denied that in one sense history from the point of view of the research specialist resembles palaeontology or archeology more than it does the experimental sciences. As Langlois[21] asserts (somewhat too broadly, as we have seen) "it is the accidental discovery of a document which suggests the idea of thoroughly elucidating the point of history to which it relates." That is to say, the process of discovery-and-explanation plays a much larger role in proportion to prediction-and-verification than is the case in the natural sciences. Consequently there is a sense in which all history rests at last upon an immense body of unrelated[22] facts, teased out of whatever documents men have chanced upon, and checked more or less carefully against the whole mass of similarly derived facts with a view simply to "getting the facts straight." It is therefore plausible to ascribe a high degree of disinterestedness to history at the research level, and then to transfer this quality to history as a school subject.

To clarify this confusion between "school history" and "historical research", it is necessary to bring the research scholar's function out into the open.

Seignobos describes the critical scholar as believing that "all historical facts have an equal right to a place in history; to retain some as being of greater importance, and reject the rest as comparatively unimportant, would be to introduce the element of choice, variable according to individual fancy; history cannot sacrifice a single fact."[23] For Seignobos, this means that, "History has the choice between two alternatives, to remain complete and unknowable, or to become knowable and incomplete."[24] In order to avoid this choice, scholars have often "preferred to confine themselves to the periods of ancient history, where chance, which has destroyed nearly all the sources of information, has freed them from the responsibility of choosing among facts by depriving them of nearly all the means of knowing them."[25]

Looked at from another angle, Seignobos' statements suggest that the critical scholar may have deliberately, and indeed quite naturally, sought out those areas within which he could use his skills most effectively. As a result, he has preferred to ground solidly a number of facts whose special value lies in the exceptional virtuosity necessary to come at them at all, rather than to try to make sense out of an imposing mass of documents whose authorship, dates, and subject-matter are clear and unquestioned.

We have, therefore, research scholars who tend to pursue, in the main, those aspects of history which allow greatest scope to their own special aptitudes; historiographers who rely for accuracy largely upon the research scholars;[26] and writers of school histories, who are occasionally professional historiographers themselves, but who are often professional educators compelled to rely largely upon the writers of general history. This set of conditions in itself should make us highly suspicious of any claim that causing students to "get the facts" is a serious concern of history teachers.

The test of the genuineness of any teacher's concern for "the facts" would be the frequency and steadiness with which pupils were urged to look behind the assertions of the text-book for the documentary or other grounding which serves as their warrant. In the writer's experience with some hundreds of teachers, only one of those who have expressed a tender concern for "the facts" and their mastery has ever revealed through overt behavior the slightest indication of disturbance over whether the materials he was "teaching" were reliable "facts" or not. Far more often, it has been clear that the teacher's basic concern was to secure obedience and a sense of power. Telling a child to "get the facts" (i.e., familiarize himself with the content of a given assignment) and then seeing that he does so by a steady application of rewards and punishments is an unusually easy way to secure the sense of making things happen.

The foregoing paragraphs are not designed to describe in detail the nature of the historical materials used in a classroom; they are intended rather to show clearly that the familiar and easy identification of "history" with "the past" is unwarranted. At the base of history is an enormous mass of statements about past events for which grounds, slender or extensive, are offered. History as written includes the products of a selection-and-exclusion process applied to such basic historical materials as the writer comes to know about, and therefore embodies the values, the purposes, and the attitudes of the writer; furthermore, the writer is compelled in the interests of sheer readability to "fill in the gaps" of his chronicle with more or less shrewd guesses whose grounds often approach zero.[27] School history, so far as "objectivity" is concerned, obviously suffers from all the foregoing limitations—it could scarcely rise above its source; but it is subject also to the variations resulting from the text-book writer's educational outlook and from the special restrictions which the publisher's conception of the market or the educator's conception of what the public will tolerate impose upon him. That which the school offers to the student, therefore, is neither "the past", nor a reliable description of "the past", nor even, so far as the course confines itself to so-called "learning of facts", a useful way of access to "the past". The alleged purpose of causing the student simply to "get the facts" is therefore at its almost inconceivable best a complete absence of purpose; ordinarily it is rather a cover for indoctrination of an exceptionally insidious kind, the general tendencies of which will be dealt with in the next chapter.

Summarizing up to this point what we have noted concerning the nature of school history, we find that:

1. The basic materials from which histories are written have been determined largely by accident.
2. The criteria guiding historiographers in their selection of content from among the basic materials are not clear.
3. The text-book writer's selection from the writings of historiographers is dictated largely by tradition.

To assume what the foregoing points may well suggest, namely, that history text-books do not embody purposes, would be unwarranted. Writers of history are not neutral, however much they may profess to be so. Ranke himself, although he wrote only what he saw as "the facts of the case", could find in what he had written a clear illustration of God's way toward man, and could see the hand of God at work even in particular events. Bancroft saw history as moving almost in a straight line toward a single goal—the creation of the America of his own day; but he insisted that his view was by no means an interpretation. It was, quite simply, a correct presentation of affairs as they really were.

Moreover, quite apart from the special predilections of individual historians, we dare not assume that tradition itself is neutral. We have seen how the conditions of the market insure a considerable uniformity among text-books with respect to factual content. This uniformity, indeed, involves no consciously held principles of selection so far as the text-book writers are concerned, but it will not do to assume on that account that no such principles are operating. On the contrary, a "traditional" body of facts means "a body of facts gathered together in terms of principles of selection which are now forgotten."

Every actual synthesis of historical materials for school use has been made with the intent to have some effect upon the beliefs, attitudes, and values of young people. The text-book writer who sees himself as setting forth "the facts" without conscious intent to affirm values or to influence attitudes merely carries on down the ages the purposes, now unstated and often forgotten, of the predecessors from whom he draws his materials.

It is obvious to the point of being tautological that one who writes history "in order to explain how we got to be as we are" must have as a starting point some notion of "how we are." He may then write to show how the hand of God brought us to our present amazing felicity, or how the institutions of capitalist society, allowing free rein to greed and callousness, have brought us to our present sorry pass. He may write, as did Vives, to show that "everything has changed and is changing every day, except the essential nature of human beings."[28] He may seek to inspire a nationalistic patriotism, not, perhaps, so naively as did the text-book writer who set himself the task of explaining, "Why are Americans the bravest men and the most successful of inventors, explorers, authors and scientists? In short, why is the United States the greatest nation in history?"[29] He may seek to furnish illustrations of virtue rewarded and wickedness punished, as Martin Luther recommended. Johnson tells us that history has been used "to illuminate the classics, to furnish recreation and entertainment, to set up examples of conduct, good and bad, to supply vicarious experiences, to offer practice in reading the human heart, to serve as a mirror in which the pupil might see himself, to support religion, to inculcate patriotism, and, in general, to build up predetermined ideals and stimulate predetermined kinds of behavior."[30]

Modern writers and teachers could not be more explicit in condemning such uses of history than was Seignobos in 1898:

> We no longer go to history for lessons in morals, nor for examples of conduct, nor yet for dramatic or picturesque scenes. We understand that for all these purposes legend would be preferable to history, for it presents a chain of causes and effects more in accordance with our ideas of justice, more perfect and heroic characters, finer and more affecting scenes. Nor do we seek to use history, as is done in Germany, for the purpose of promoting patriotism and loyalty; we felt that it would be illogical for different persons to draw opposite conclusions from the same science according to their country or party; it would be an invitation to every people to mutilate, if not to alter history in the direction of its pref-

erences. We understand that the value of every science consists in its being true, and we ask from history truth and nothing more.[31]

Seignobos's colleague, Langlois, makes a sly commentary on these brave words in a footnote:

> Let it be noted, however, that to the question, "What purpose is served by the teaching of history," eighty per cent of the candidates [for the modern Baccalaureate in 1897] answered, in effect, either because they believed it or because they thought it would please, "to promote patriotism."[32]

Our attempt to get a clue to a meaning for the expression "teaching history" by an examination of what "history" has meant, in school and out, seems to have struck a blank wall. We get a sense that historical materials are so called not because of any intrinsic "historicity", but by virtue of their having become known through the application of techniques belonging to what is called "historical method"; that this method enables us to impute a degree of "reality" to historical materials which we do not attribute to novels or to legends; and that this quality should somehow render historical materials useful in coping with today's problems. We have seen that history has been used in schools for a wide variety of purposes, and that there is nothing in the materials of history which suggests the purposes that history ought to serve. We have seen that an uncritical attempt to teach history as if its present traditional content were "the past" simply perpetuates the differing and often conflicting interpretations of the historiographers upon whom the text-book writer relies for his content.

One fact, however, has been established in this chapter: it is quite impossible to write or to teach history simply "for its own sake", or "to give the children the facts." It is impossible because there is neither a body of materials identifiable as "history", nor any clue within the facts themselves as to which ones are *the* facts.

History can be written and taught in such a way as to produce definite and to some extent predictable results within the experience of students; but we cannot find out from an examination of history what history is good for. The answer to that question must be sought within the social outlook of the person who seeks to answer it. If that person's deepest allegiances are to one or another of the many authoritarian value-patterns now operating in the world, he will make a response appropriate to his pattern. If his central loyalty is to the democratic ideal, his response will be of a different character, and perhaps of a different order. Certain implications of the democratic ideal for the teaching of history will be treated in the next chapter.

III
SOME IMPLICATIONS OF
THE DEMOCRATIC IDEAL

We have seen that the nature of historical subject matter provides neither clues as to how it ought to be used nor guarantees as to how it will be used. Yet the idea that history is an entity with an office to perform, and that an increase in the time devoted to the study of history will produce predictable and beneficent results, is continually reasserted from all kinds of sources. The haste with which states passed legislation requiring high school courses in American history during and just after World War I should have led us to expect a similar naive but well-intended movement in connection with World War II. That a professor of history[33] should place himself in the front ranks of those who see in more and longer required courses a solution to the problem of preparing for democratic citizenship is more surprising.

Professor Nevins expresses a concern for the fact that "twenty-two states have no real history requirement," and sees in legislation for the teaching of American history a remedy for the difficulties pointed out by an undergraduate whom he quotes as saying, "Year after year the majority of young men go into the world without a very deep faith and conviction in the democratic way of life."

Professor Nevins, perhaps for reasons of space, does not touch upon what he sees as the connection between courses in American history and a faith in the democratic way of life. He is indignant over the fact that young Americans "know something about Alexander Hamilton but are not quite sure of Albert Gallatin; they have heard of Harriet Beecher Stowe, but not of Hinton R. Helper; ....they are uncertain whether Polk came before Pierce, Irving before Herman Melville, or McCormick before Alexander Graham Bell."

What Professor Nevins does not show, how-ever, includes three propositions that are necessary to make his case. He does not show, in the first place, what reason there is for believing that faith and conviction in the democratic way of life would be strengthened if students knew all about both Gallatin and Helper, and could recite the presidents backwards, with dates. He does not show, in the second place, that his charges of ignorance are valid only for students who have grown up in those states where the American history requirement is "inadequate"; indeed, the tenor of his article suggests that they are intended to have nation-wide application. He does not show, in the third place, how faith in democracy managed to survive the long years when almost no American history was taught—the very years which much of today's history will necessarily be about.

It is certainly no part of the purpose of the present study to take issue with Professor Nevins on the value of American history, or on the importance of keeping the nation's faith in democracy steady and firm. The issue is simply whether "more history" can safely be recommended as a remedy without some notation on the prescription as to what it is and how it is to be taken. The danger in the proposal is precisely the danger that attends the recommendation of a harmless patent medicine; the patient is lulled into security about a serious condition because he is "taking something" for it.

One assumption which would give meaning to Nevin's approach (an assumption which, as a historian, he assuredly does not make) is that American history illustrates in all its parts the steady effort of a whole people to apply the test of the democratic ideal to all phases of living. If this assumption were warranted, there would be some reason to hope that the child, finding democracy all about him and discovering it also as the uniform tradition of his country, would simply "catch on", and come at democracy without difficulty or confusion. But if the assumption were warranted, the problem to which Nevins' proposal is addressed would not now exist.

The central thesis of the history teacher has always been that, wherever we now are, we got there as a result of what occurred in the past. It follows that, so far as Nevins is correct in the opinion that our young people do not have adequate faith and conviction in the democratic way of life, the reasons for this unhappy condition will be a part of any history which professes to explain the important aspects of our present living. And if we hold, as Nevins obviously does, that the general trend of American living has been essentially democratic, it is clear that only the presence in our midst of profoundly undemocratic and very powerful forces could account for the condition of the public mind which Nevins' recommendation is designed to remedy. In that case, we can scarcely hope to instill a faith in democracy simply by pointing to the American tradition and saying, "That's it." The very conditions alleged to show the need for such a procedure furnish the best possible evidence of its inadequacy.

What is needed, clearly, is analysis of our tradition, rather than a sheer pointing to it. We need to know what we mean by democracy, and we need to ground that knowledge as widely and as richly as possible. We need not merely to get acquainted with our culture, but to make judgments about it in terms of the democratic ideal. By so doing, we hope to secure not only facility in applying the democratic ideal as a test in judgments of practice, but also a control of materials likely to be particularly useful in applying the democratic test to "the quandaries of present-day living."

Indeed, it is entirely possible, so far as any evidence now available is concerned, to believe that an uncritical acquaintance with American history, accompanied by the suggestion, "This is your tradition, and you must be loyal to it," would only increase that lack of clear commitment to democracy by which Nevins is very properly disturbed. A tradition which, as presented, seems to underwrite indiscriminately the activities and ideas of Jefferson and Hamilton, Lincoln and Stanton, Calhoun and Jackson, is almost certain to leave any thoughtful student with the question, "What is that to which I am committed by a loyalty to the American tradition?"

For the teacher of history, the problem becomes in part one of developing in the student the capacity to make the kind of analysis that is needed, and in part one of helping him, so far as that may be necessary, to make it. Some hypotheses as to how these two things could perhaps be done make up the content of chapter six. Inasmuch as anything history teachers may decide to do in this connection will necessarily involve on the teacher's part a clear understanding of what democracy means, and will also be subject on its own account to the democratic test, the present chapter will center upon the meaning of the democratic ideal as a test for judgments of practice.

The concept of democracy, like all other concepts, was carved out of human experience, rather than invented *a priori* or built into the original structure of the universe. That is to say, the idea of democracy had to be made up as a meaning for things that men found themselves doing before anybody could *intend* to act in terms of democracy as an ideal.

In its early forms, democracy seems to have involved little more than the idea of membership; whoever "belonged" to a group had a right to some "say" in what the group decided to do, and was expected to accept a share in doing it. During a great part of the existence of Athens as a city-state, for example, a citizen could make himself felt through his vote and through the exercise of his influence; he shared in the effort toward common goals by his participation in the activities of one or more of the many committees, chosen by lot, through which the

Athenians carried on public business; he served on huge juries; he was expected to perform military service, and to have a voice in naming his general. He could, indeed, be banished for purely political reasons, as was Aristides, or even executed for holding and teaching what were regarded as objectionable opinions, as was Socrates; but these things would be done neither by an irresponsible mob nor by a capricious monarch. They would be done by his peers, his fellow-citizens, acting through their organized institutions, with due process of law. In the vernacular, everybody got about the same breaks, took about the same risks, and was "in on" almost everything. Obviously, whatever of democracy Athens enjoyed was strictly a class affair; metics and slaves, who together made up most of the population, were not within its purview. Moreover, we are learning that the hand of custom was heavy even over Athens, so that individual freedom was enjoyed within fairly narrow limits. Nevertheless, a relatively large group of people had a good deal to say about the decisions which affected their living, and equality within the group was taken for granted.

On some scale, large or small, all societies about which we know anything at all have afforded opportunities for participation to some proportion of the people operating within them. Almost everyone got at least a taste of participation—even slaves, in interaction with other slaves or with a family to whom they were attached, could in some degree make themselves felt, and have a part in the determination of what happened. It is reasonably safe to say that whenever people live in any kind of association with others, some degree of participation for each individual is inevitable. Its limits, however, may be extremely narrow.

The factors which can shut men off from all but a tiny share in the common interests and common concerns of the society within which they live are three in number:

(1) A so-called aristocracy, maintained either by tradition, or by naked force, or by skillful engineering of consent, or by all of these means, may monopolize such opportunities for participation as the culture affords.

(2) The culture itself may be so completely dominated by fixed standards with whose establishment no living man has been concerned that nearly all action can be carried on in terms simply of what is "correct" or what is "taboo". In this case, full membership status in a dominant group may still provide only a modicum of participation.

(3) Whole masses of people, by reason of physical inheritance, nurture, or both, may be incapable of utilizing the opportunities for participation which the culture affords.

All three of these barriers to participation are inter-related. Ruling classes make use of the tradition wherever it buttresses their control and sanctions their values; through propaganda and other controls they make use of underdeveloped sections of the population, both as a tool in securing their ends and as an argument against opening up the culture to all men. The inability of men shut off from wide participation to see their own interests clearly is a factor which sustains the ruling class in power. The tradition, insofar as it prescribes specific behaviors or reinforces specific values, serves to keep both men and classes unmodified, because it actually reduces the range of possible participation for everyone. Indeed, it is possible for the tradition to secure such power that men of all classes are at its mercy and human development almost comes to a halt. Long stretches may be pulled out of the history of Egypt or of Sparta, to show, not men at the mercy of other men who deliberately make use of existing institutions and customs, but rather *all* men at the mercy of institutions and customs in whose creation they had no part.

Participation could be defined as the finding of meanings in what one is doing, and the direction of one's activity, at least in part, by the meanings he has found. The grounding of the argument at the basis of most "great man" theories of history, namely, that the exceptional man has participated far more effectively in human affairs than have many millions of common men taken all together, is equally susceptible of the explanation, "Those who have had or made the opportunity for wide participation have developed into exceptional men."

The democratic ideal has been formulated in many ways, by many men; it is susceptible of many formulations as we emphasize now one aspect and now another. But the every-day, operational meaning of democracy in America, and the meaning we tend to emphasize whenever we are reacting off-hand rather than straining for precise language, is the "being-in-on-things" meaning, the "having-a-say" meaning.

Ordinarily, men have not often taken as a goal the securing for everyone of opportunities for participation. In America, an able man was supposed to be able to secure such opportunities for himself. And it is no wonder that America, with its incredibly rapid growth, its moving frontier, its freedom from any highly specific over-all tradition, was able to provide a considerable degree of participation for any man who was willing to make a try for it. Because of a combination of accidental and highly favorable circumstances, the efforts of individual men to secure maximum participation for themselves resulted in a set of social arrangements which, until about 1890, provided very wide opportunities to substantially all men except Negroes and Indians. So long as government kept hands off, individuals and groups could maintain their own right to participate, to make themselves count, to be considered. The result was an inordinate reliance on "freedom"; given freedom, men could look after equality for themselves. And they did so again and again, whenever signs began to appear indicating that any appreciable group was being cut off from a fair share in the common enterprise that was America. By actual violence or by threat of violence, by popular uprisings under Jefferson, Jackson, and Lincoln, men whose guiding principle was not much

more than "Everyone must protect his own rights" happened (rather than managed) to keep conditions of freedom and equality open wider, for more people, and for a longer time than ever before in history.

There is no need to repeat here that the conditions which gave us democracy as a fact, without our needing to *intend* it, are no longer widely operative. Professor Craven[34] has described the problem we face as concisely as possible:

Freedom under urban industrialism had proved to be something else. It had too often meant freedom to exploit and to lift the few above the many. It had produced America's first real aristocracy. Slums and share-croppers and class hatred had become a normal part of national life.

If democracy was to live, the emphasis had to shift from freedom to the other ingredient of the dogma, equality. If men were to be equal, however, they could no longer achieve equality for themselves. Government would have to become more active. Democracy would be a choice from then on. It would have to be planned if it were to continue to exist. And all this in the face of strong men, also born out of the American experience, who had no interest or desire for either freedom or equality for anyone except themselves. Somehow or other a balance would have to be made. That was the new problem facing a people who had never even taken the trouble to define democracy or to inquire into its meaning either as a theory or as a practice in American life.

Seen against the background of Professor Craven's incisive and realistic words, proposals to teach more history, or to tinker a bit with the usual content, or to find more plausibly phrased objectives, suggest that their framers are either optimistic enough to think that our present colossal difficulties will somehow "work themselves out", or else thoroughly pessimistic about the power of school history to make any real difference in the outcome.

If we want to teach history in such a way as to make a difference on the side of democracy, it is not enough (although it has helped, and will help) simply to increase the opportunities of students for participation in the activities of the classroom or the life of the school. Indeed, if that were our single purpose, it would be hard to justify bothering with history at all. In order to locate the implications of the democratic ideal for the teaching of history, we shall need to return to a consideration of the factors which now impede the participation of the common man in the life about him.

We have said that these factors are three: the existence of a ruling class, the limitations imposed by tradition upon the subject-matter of participation, and the limited capacities for participation of some of our people.

No one will deny the appropriateness of the school's concern for the third of these difficulties; as a result, lists of objectives for every subject in the curriculum express an interest in promoting reflective thinking, or a scientific attitude, or a reliance on the method of intelligence. The present writer is willing to agree that in the long run the development of the student's capacity for independent reflection is the school's special contribution to the democratic way of life. But he does not believe that the school can focus its sights simply upon that purpose, unless it is expressed in terms which leave no doubt of its intended universality of application, and which make that universality an integral part of the purpose.

As matters now stand, most of us give at least lip-service to the idea that students should learn to interpret data of many kinds, to apply principles in new situations, to suggest ways for checking and testing hypotheses, to construct a logical proof, to spot unstated assumptions, to set up and perform experiments. These activities seem well calculated to develop in young people a realization that reflection, or scientific method, is *a* way of determining truth. But what is needed in the present world, if democracy as a way of life is to have a fighting chance for survival, is a reliance upon reflection, not as *a* method, but as *the* method for determining the truth of any proposition about any subject whatever.

Not even the Nazis would deny the validity of reflection as *a* method; they have merely extended beyond what some of us regard as endurable limits the areas which their fixed tradition has arrogated to itself as no longer appropriate for inquiry.

Reflection as a useful tool needs neither friends nor defenders; no society that refused to employ it could survive for a month. It is childish to deceive ourselves or our students with the proposition, "Totalitarian states don't think; democracies do." A more adequate formulation would be, "Societies are democratic, in terms of one possible test, to the degree to which they refrain from setting limits upon the matters that may be thought about." The effort to serve the ends of democracy by increasing the capacity of the individual for participation thus brings us almost at once up against a partly-authoritarian tradition that cries out for critical examination.

The same thing happens if we approach our problem through a consideration of the ruling class as a factor limiting participation. In America, no one publicly claims membership in the ruling class, or asserts special privileges for it as a matter of right. Nor does a sharp line, either of income or of profession, mark off the ruling class from the rest of the population. The class makes itself felt largely through associations and through control of the agencies that influence public opinion; it is probable that in the main individual members see themselves as fighting only for their rights, as these are outlined in our tradition. The small group who seem to know what they are doing are extremely careful to rely upon well-loved and ostensibly "democratic" aspects of the tradition, such as "individual freedom", or "the right to work", rather than upon claims of aristocracy, in their efforts to consolidate their position. The "laws of economics", the "tenets of true religion", or the "lessons of history" bulk large in their armory.

A head-on attack against this amorphous group is, as of today, quite impossible. Anyone who attempted it would be hit hard on both flanks by the forces of tradition, and would probably be annihilated before he could even reach the stage of clearly identifying his enemy. Moreover, there is reason to believe that, without the protection afforded by those aspects of our own tradition which inhibit participation, the "ruling class" in America would prove to be a tiny and a feeble aggregation.

The clear point of attack, as of today, upon the forces inimical to democracy, is therefore upon the authoritarian aspects of our American tradition. However, because our purpose is finally to foster democracy, our procedures must be carefully chosen. Hitler has shown that it is possible thoroughly to smash one set of authoritarian principles and customs by the device of imposing another set. No such procedure can serve the ends of democracy. The question of devising appropriate methods is dealt with at some length in succeeding chapters; it is enough here to enter a disclaimer on the intent to advocate "indoctrination for democracy."

What are the areas of our tradition within which the method of reflection is not freely permitted to operate? Two areas stand out as almost invariably resistant to examination, namely, economics (especially in its relation to class conflict) and religion. These two are not always related to each other. Three more areas which are protected by varying thicknesses or armor in various sections and class groups are those involving race, nationalism, and sex customs. However, the taboos surrounding all three of these areas have been worn down considerably in the past decade alone.

The American tradition with regard to religion is a confusion twice confounded. In the first place, we have our vaunted principles of "religious tolerance", which have rested largely upon the prohibition laid upon Congress by the first amendment and upon similar provisions in state constitutions. Religion was free from governmental controls, so long as no other strongly entrenched conviction was violated by a given religious group. The Mormons quickly learned what happens to religion that runs afoul of sex mores, and Jehovah's Witnesses know by now not only that religious freedom must not contravene the principle of nationalism, but also that a guarantee against interference by government is no protection against the arrogance of the self-appointed custodians of public welfare who can generally be recruited from public loafing-places. The Witnesses themselves, of course, display a similar arrogance toward the Catholic Church and all its works, although they confine themselves to blatant manifestations of bad taste, rather than resorting to violence.

For the most part, the inability of any one sect to gain a dominant position in America has meant that all are committed, for the sake of sheer self-preservation, to a policy of mutual forbearance which in no sense involves any yielding of the claim to be the true religion, or one of a small group of true religions. Religious freedom has guaranteed the right of each parent, so far as he cares to and is able, to prevent his child from exercising any freedom in this area. Discussion of religion is generally held to be in bad taste; it is usually prohibited (although in small, homogeneous Protestant communities it may also be virtually required) in the public schools. The peculiar effect of religious freedom, thus conceived, is to lift those aspects of experience generally associated with the concept "religious" almost bodily out of daily living in order to "protect" them. Religious ideas, carefully wrapped, are stored in the attic, and our common living is thereby tragically impoverished. On the other hand, so far as religions profess to embody divinely revealed truths, inter-action among them can only result in flat counterclaims with no possibility of adjustment. And to allow children, before they have become callous, to discover that revelations differ is to cast doubt upon the validity of revelation as a method for securing truth.

In addition to the peculiar state of affairs growing out of a multiplicity of religions, all claiming to possess absolute truth whose grounds, lying outside ordinary experience, are not subject to examination, we have also the inherent conflict within the Christian religion itself. We have the authoritarian concept of God as a father-image, handing down fixed rules from Mount Sinai and imposing cruel and unusual punishments upon all who fail to nourish his apparently unlimited self-esteem. On the other hand, we have Jesus of Nazareth, who defied the tradition of his day, altered the concept of God far more violently than Hosea, or Micah, or Isaiah had altered it, denied the validity of an explicit pronouncement by Moses on divorce, and even challenged the ten commandments with his bold and incisive assertion, "The Sabbath was made for man, not man for the Sabbath."

We have, then, two conflicting principles operating within Christianity: the authoritarian principle that God is all, controls everything, and has made mankind for inscrutable purposes of his own; and the democratic principles that human brotherhood has significance, that the human personality is important, and that even the rules of religion are to be tested in terms of their effect upon human development. Obviously, one can find sanction for almost anything in a religion thus conceived; one may be cruel and self-righteous in the name of the Father that sent bears to devour the boys who laughed at the prophet, or he may condone what some would call aberrant behavior in the name of the Son who comforted the Magdalen.

It is well to remember that Germany and Italy grew up in the Christian tradition, too. They have sloughed off one part of that tradition—the democratic teachings of Jesus. They have kept, and used up to the hilt, the authoritarian view that men who claim to lead by virtue of special and untestable insight or revelation are to be taken seriously. They have kept also the ideas that submissiveness to a higher will is a virtue, that leadership properly flows from the top down, in the form of arbitrary orders, and that to apply ordinary tests for truth to formulations offered on sufficiently high authority is to be wicked, presumptuous, and lacking in faith.

Nazis and Fascists have secured a clear position on this question: the way to get truth on questions relating to basic values is to accept it on authority, without doubt or testing. We in America have no such clarity. In most areas we readily accept reflection as the method for determining truth; but in selected areas, of which religion is one, we underwrite both the method of revelation and the method of intelligence as it was invoked by Jesus and earlier Jewish prophets.

Obviously, anyone's claim to be inspired or to have control of the truth by special and unexaminable methods may be handled either by the ordinary tests of experience or by taking the claimant solely on his word. There is a world of difference between accepting Jones's statement tentatively, for use in action, because it sounds reasonable, or because Jones is in a position to know about such matters, and accepting Jones's statement because Jones is a special kind of man who gets and deals in an untestable truth which is exempt from the obligation to meet the ordinary tests of experience.

A democratic society can make terms with an authoritarian religion only by relegating the ethical and moral questions with which religion is concerned to a very limited role in our culture. To our loss, that is what has happened. People who take their authoritarian religion seriously must withdraw even from such common enterprises as the public school. Otherwise, they run afoul of vaccination requirements, flag salutes, moving pictures, dancing, or other activities which by one or another standard are just plain wrong for reasons unrelated to their probable consequences.

It is impossible as well as pointless to deny the numerous and valuable contributions to democracy that have been made by church groups and by churchmen. After all, democratic tendencies constitute one aspect of both Christianity and Judaism. But both of these dispensations date from a time when there was no clear alternative to authoritarianism. Part of the school's problem, then, must be to attempt to bring back into the every-day world the ethical and moral concerns which have been tied to authoritarianism and withdrawn into the realm of the unexaminable.

In the area of economics, the need is clearly for a critical examination of our business system not only in terms of the democratic ideal, but also in the light of the principles under which the system is alleged to operate, and in the light of the needs of our people and of the world. Young people are obviously entitled to examine and to judge the ways in which our society carries on the production and distribution of goods and services. They are entitled also to some help in looking behind the sacred ideas of "the open market," "free enterprise," "competition," and "laissez-faire," none of which business in America has shown any desire to use as guides for practice within many decades, and to discern the combination of eighteenth century mercantilist theory and monopoly by agreement that actually seems to direct the behaviors of Chambers of Commerce and trade associations. That American business, having obliterated almost every trace of free capitalist enterprise, should have been able steadily to appear as the defender of its own long-dead victim is one of the most remarkable contradictions in the weird confusion of American economic theory. In particular, however, young people are entitled to understand, and to appraise in the light of the democratic ideal, that concept of ownership which asserts for the owners, or for a management presumed to act in the owners' interests, a monopoly of participation in the control and direction of the firm's business, no matter how many other people may be directly affected by any decisions that are taken.

Assuredly, the school has no business to indoctrinate a loyalty to any competing system of economic organization; the task of the democratic school is to make the student intelligent about his culture, rather than to win his adherence to predetermined courses of action. But if we are sincere in our commitment to democracy, we should no more hesitate to call attention to the authoritarian aspects of business than we would hesitate to call attention to the evils of government by political bosses or the unhappy consequences of a contaminated water-supply. Moreover, a part of any critical examination of our economic system will include the consideration of measures that might be adopted in the interests of a democratization of business. Many students in secondary schools would find in such writers as J. A. Hobson, Stuart Chase, or John Strachey a highly fertile source of suggestions to be tested; exceptional students might profitably examine the ideas of Marx and Engels. There is no imaginable reason, so far as democracy is concerned, for withholding any relevant material from any student capable of being informed by it. And no one who is familiar with the ideas of Karl Marx will share the apparent fear of many American businessmen that those ideas are so clear and so invulnerable to criticism as to win the acceptance of everyone who is allowed to examine them.

The same principles hold for other "touchy" areas. No reasonable man will ask others to act upon the belief that different races are inherently unequal in cultural capacities, and at the same time insist that the belief in question must not be examined. That many of our states have created social arrangements which pander to the prejudices of one part of their population at the expense of the participation of another part is not merely a scandalous contravention of the democratic ideal, but an actual military asset to the forces of authoritarianism in Burma, in India, and to some extent throughout the world. We are learning that nations which tolerate a withholding from minority races of the opportunity for full and free participation are likely to call in vain upon those races for help in the name of democracy.

It is not within the scope of this chapter, or indeed of this study, to undertake the kind of analysis that needs to be made by students as they move toward an understanding of American culture and the American tradition. The present chapter is designed simply to indicate some of the directions which such an analysis must take, if we accept as our central purpose the task of helping young people toward an understanding of their own way of life and a conscious choice between democracy and authoritarianism as guiding principles.

For anyone who does not see as the school's major task the development of young people into men and women who are capable of effective participation in democratic living, and who are capable also of steadily recreating, consciously and purposefully, the conditions which make democratic living possible, the subsequent chapters of this study will have no force. They attempt nothing more than to explore the implications of the foregoing commitment, first in regard to the teaching of history, and then in regard to the subject-matter preparation of history teachers. If the commitment itself is held to be unacceptable, the following chapters are almost exactly as useful as a Pennsylvania road map in California. That is to say, they will perhaps yield an inference or two, but their over-all value will be negligible.

IV
THE UNIQUE FUNCTION OF
INFORMATION IN A DEMOCRACY

A detailed treatment of the nature of the learning process, or of the theories of learning which have at various times and places sanctioned or given rise to educational practices is beyond the scope of the present study. On the other hand, it is impossible to write about the teaching of history out of reference to a conception of the nature of learning.

It is interesting to observe in passing that our familiar conception of school learning suffers from almost exactly the same difficulties as does our familiar conception of history (see Chapter II). Just as "history" can be called "what is taught in history classes," so learning may be, and often is, defined as "what children do in school." But "what children do in school" is the result of a handing down of practices which were at some time seen as implementing some theory of learning. Exercises for the faculties of will, memory, reason, etc., are no longer so called, because "faculty psychology" has been exploded; but the exercises go on, ordinarily because "that's what you do in school" rather than because anyone seriously believes in the educational theory by which the practices were once sanctioned. The bodies of subject-matter to be digested by means of the five formal steps, because subject-matters so digested were seen as adding to and combining with the apperceptive mass and thus not merely improving, but actually constituting the mind of the student, are still with us, although the formal steps survive only in the habits of a few older teachers and the theory of mental states survives not at all.

Again like history, the study of the learning process has been profoundly affected by the tendency of research specialists to seek out for investigation those areas which give greatest scope to their skills and techniques. As a consequence, although no one seriously challenges the proposition that "from the time of Socrates, the intellectual life of the Western world, its sciences and its philosophies, as well as its practical enterprises, have rested on the integrity of the concept as the irreducible unit of reflective thought,"[35] educational psychology has been relatively perfunctory in its investigations of the reflective process. The comparatively easy amenability of habit formation, or perceptual-motor learning, to the more precise techniques of the experimental psychologist has attracted workers in droves. Like research specialists in history, they have asked, not "What is important?" but rather, "Where can I most fully employ my special powers and capacities? Where can I best do my stuff?" One well-known educational psychologist,[36] in 1938, listed three major investigations of the reflective process: Dewey's "How We Think", James Harvey Robinson's "The Mind in the Making", and Piaget's "Child's Conception of the World." Of the latter she suggests some disagreement among psychologists as to its significance. It is significant that neither Dewey nor Robinson is known primarily as a psychologist, and that the books in question are respectively thirty and twenty years old.

Almost every standard work in the field of psychology contains a chapter or a section devoted to what is called "the learning process." These chapters usually pay at least passing respects to the reflective process, but in the main they are devoted to careful descriptions of elaborately instituted and controlled procedures which evoke more or less persistent modifications in the behavior of organisms.

It seems fair to say, in view of the lengths to which experimental psychologists go to insure that no *unintended* learning slips in to confuse their experiments, that psychology has been concerned not so much with the learning process as with the outcomes of a variety of "teaching" processes; it seeks to investigate those behavior-outcomes which may be attributed to particular modifications of the environment. Psychologists ordinarily try to investigate, by the techniques with which science is familiar, *those learnings which they themselves have deliberately produced*, in one clearly described way or another. Obviously, only perceptual motor learnings or involuntary physiological reactions can easily be handled on these terms. Psychologists may, indeed, twist and turn their deliberately produced outcomes about in a bewildering variety of ways, measuring the speed with which intended responses are acquired, or how long they persist, or what influence various changes in procedure will have upon rate of "learning", retention, etc., or the influence of specified affective qualities of the materials "studied", or "the galvanic skin deflections elicited upon the presentation of various affective words."

The meticulous precision and elaborate care that characterize these studies may be illustrated by the following examples, chosen quite at random from a huge mass of very similar materials, which supply, by implication, an interesting answer to the question, "What is meant by learning?"

You have in the apparatus before you ten rows of bolts with ten bolts in a row. The rows are lettered from A to J and the bolts in each row are numbered from 1 to 10. One bolt in each row, and only one, is connected in such a way that the buzzer will sound when the correct circuit is made. That is, each letter is assigned a number in a random order from 1 to 10. This number is the one that will cause the buzzer to sound when the bolt is touched. No two letters have the same number.

Your problem is to begin with row A and find the bolt that will cause the buzzer to sound. Then go to row B and find the bolt there that will sound the buzzer, and

so on through the entire series from A to J. Now go back to row A and repeat the process. Continue repeating the process until you go from A to J twice in succession without making an error.[37]

A second quotation reveals a conception of the nature of learning almost identical with the one illustrated above:

The stimulus cards contained the same forms as those in the later research, but in different combinations, the forms being set at distances of eight degrees from the fixation point. Each card was exposed for one-tenth of a second. The subjects were instructed, as in the other experiments, that we wanted "to see how much, and how readily they could learn to apprehend forms beyond the normal range of distinct vision."[38]

One more illustration should suffice to give the flavor of the kind of thing an investigator unearths in profusion when he undertakes to discover what has been written on the general subject of "The Learning Process."

The purpose of this investigation was to study the interrelationships of the following factors: (1) the affective value of the materials used in learning; (2) the volitional attitude assumed during learning; (3) the efficiency of learning; and (4) the galvanic skin deflections elicited upon the presentation of the materials.

The general method of approach to this problem was as follows: Subjects were presented with lists of words that contained paired associates of a pleasant, unpleasant and indifferent character. They were instructed to assume either an active or a passive attitude while learning a list. Each list was presented but once, and recall followed immediately after presentation. The efficiency of learning was measured in terms of the number of items recalled and the speed of recall. Measures of the maximum magnitudes of the galvanic skin reflex deflections elicited during learning were obtained.[39]

It is certainly not the purpose of the present writer to deny the significance or possible utility of the particular studies from which the foregoing excerpts are quoted. Such studies help to provide an answer for one very practical question, namely: "If we know what habits we want people to acquire, how can we most efficiently bring about their acquisition?"

The utility of such studies for secondary school teachers in a democracy is very real, although they certainly do not provide useful suggestions for method. Their usefulness is rather in acquainting teachers with the measurable effectiveness of devices, techniques, and procedures intended to elicit specific behaviors or to develop specific habits.

Obviously, an individual may want to develop certain specific habits, in which case it is desirable that he know how. He may even want help in developing them very quickly, and it is therefore desirable to have people around who can help him. The disquieting consideration, however, is that people who know how may feel impelled, from all sorts of motives, to develop specific habits in other people quite apart from any purpose of the subject or victim.

The thoroughly established fact that by fully controlling the environment of a child we can alter the nature of his habitual responses with amazingly little difficulty, plus the fairly clear evidence that adults continue indefinitely to be capable of this kind of "learning", helps us to see vividly the major threat of authoritarianism to our way of life. We see the polar devices of "Kraft durch Freude" and concentration camps as resting upon a sound and judicious application of the Law of Effect. We see the casual greeting, "Heil, Hitler"—which was funny once—as an example of the Law of Use. We see poor, aging Petain struggling desperately to "re-educate" the French people by a shift in the bases of rewards and punishments. But we see also that *in a democracy, no educational system can place its major reliance upon learning as habit formation.*

A process in which some people develop what they conceive to be desirable specific habits in other people may well be justified in the early years of the elementary school and in certain cases even later. Such a process would presumably be directed toward insuring the health, safety, or comfort of the child and of those around him, and would make no pretense of being educative. Carried beyond this point, it could only interfere with the child's capacity for participation and with his development of self-direction.

Even if this were not true, and if there were no basic antithesis between democracy and the conditioning of the responses of individuals capable of finding and choosing their own responses, the process of inculcating specific habits would be a slender reed to lean on in preparing students for life.

No matter how successfully we might equip the child in school with the habits we wanted him to have, the extra-school environment would always (more or less rapidly in proportion to the student's "adaptability") wreck the complex of habits we had built up. The kind of behavior that "pays off" in school gets learned for school, and then is replaced by the kind of behavior that "pays off" in adult life. Of course, the school environment can be intentionally organized to develop "desirable" habits, while the adult's environment is not (in a democracy) rigidly organized for habit-forming purposes by a single, unified agency external to the individual. But the purposes of commercial advertisers, pressure groups, and political organizations, to name only a few striking examples, are in a sense identical in kind with the purposes of habit-formation (in other people) anywhere. Habit is behavior that has become relatively automatic, and that kind of behavior brings cash into the till, or votes into the ballot box, for anyone who can skillfully manipulate the environment of his fellow-man in terms of the laws of so-called learning. It follows that, even if the teacher had some sure touchstone for determining in every case what habitual responses are desirable,[40] he would still be helpless in the face of the fact that the student can learn *new* habits in precisely the same way in which he learned the earlier and (putatively) desirable habits. The child who has become habitually sensitive to the interests of others, not through any concern of his own, but merely because that kind of behavior enables him to "get along" in his school environment, can just as readily "learn", in adult life, to drop the portcullis of his soul and stare out icily from behind it, holding aloft a banner inscribed, "After all, business is business."

If we were to regard education as primarily a matter of habit-formation, we should need to choose from a very limited list of alternatives in order to make our work effective. One way would be to get control not merely of the schools, but of our whole society, and then to see to it that the habits we have lovingly inculcated actually do find their reward. The brutality (as of today) of turning loose in the world a youngster who has developed, for example, unexamined habits of free association with members of other races would then alter its quality because the whole society would have been conditioned to similar habits. The problem of how to get control of society would, of course, be a large one, and the difficulty of building concentration camps extensive enough to house that part of the adult population which resisted all our treatments could well prove insuperable. It is unlikely that anyone would presume seriously to entertain the purpose of conditioning all of society to operate in ways that would make the conditioning given by schools appropriate. The possibility is at least logically present, however; and some of its consequences, projected in imagination (e.g., Governor Talmadge of Georgia in process of being conditioned to habits of racial tolerance) are aesthetically gratifying.

A second arrangement which would make the theory of learning as habit-formation func-

tional would be to ascertain what habits are acceptable to those who now largely control the instrumentalities of adult habit-formation, and then to inculcate these habits in the schools. Obviously, only generalized habits would be admissible (for example, children could be taught to use a patented dentifrice, rather than the equally efficacious salt or soda; but schools could not do the whole job for any single manufacturer, except in cases of clear monopoly). In this way, the habits of the whole population would in some degree be made to dovetail, and a groundwork would be laid for the apotheosis of our common habits into some sort of mystical what-is-it about which could be built the Fascism that alone could hold such a learning-structure together. That this kind of outcome is entirely possible, and that something very like it has often occurred, no student of the history of education can doubt. But America, by the grace of that Providence which gave us for generations a moving frontier and a steady influx of immigrants, is by now so incorrigibly pluralistic in its value patterns that it probably "can't happen here."

If the foregoing elaborations of the theory of learning as the drilling in of predetermined habits appear fantastic, it is because the theory itself, when applied to secondary education, seems to the writer to be fantastic; or, rather, to be worthy of the name "fantastic" if only it possessed that internal logic which readers ordinarily demand even in fantasy. For if the "conditioner" who is drilling habits into children has no better reason for preferring these habits than his own prior conditioning, the whole process depends for its grounding upon the fortuitous value-patterns of some prior conditioner who is himself "uneducated", while if the "conditioner" *does* have a more valid basis for the selection of what habits to inculcate than his own "conditioning", the need to develop *that kind* of basis in the child would appear to be a clear implication of the position, as well as a clear contradiction of it, and for this reason to reduce the position itself to absurdity.[41]

If the role of education in a democracy cannot be simply the inculcation of specific habits or attitudes, what then? The purpose of this chapter is to emphasize the unique role, in a democracy, of that kind of learning into which information enters and out of which it is generated. The emphasis, naturally enough, will be upon the function of the teacher inside this process.

The most obvious statement of the teacher's function (qua teacher) is that he should foster learning on the part of his students. Any society in which teachers exist and are recognized as teachers would accept this formulation. To say more than this—even to make the meaning of the verb "to learn" more explicit—is possible only within the framework of a social philosophy.

A totalitarian state (as the most extreme example of authoritarian control) may take the position that the teacher ought to cause students (1) to adopt or "take on" certain very specific attitudes; (2) to develop a number of fairly specific habits acquired through a multitude of prescribed activities; (3) to accept the orthodox pattern of beliefs and values, in terms of which the approved habits and attitudes fit together and make sense; and (4) to become aware of a body of facts carefully selected (or myths carefully constructed) to give evidential support to the accepted set of beliefs.

There is nothing vague or even very difficult about preparing teachers for so clearly defined a task as the foregoing; only the question of methods has any element of indeterminacy, and even here evaluation is so simplified by the clear and unequivocal character of the objectives that results of research can be handed on quite directly to practitioners, somewhat as in the field of medicine, without urgent need to make them understand the process through which the "better way" was developed and tested.

Education (and therefore teacher preparation) may be made thus simple and efficient whenever a society is prepared to set forth a hierarchy of preferred values and habits, a col-

lection of unquestionable beliefs, a set of orthodox attitudes, and a selection of "things children ought to know" (a term which as here used is intended to suggest recognition and deliberate suppression of its opposite, "things children ought *not* to know"). Individuals are not lacking in America who are prepared to do precisely this thing, often in the name of democracy itself; fortunately, they tend at the moment to cancel each other out. They disagree sharply with one another upon the appropriate specific content for each of the foregoing categories, and each can see that to allow the other fellow to put *his* program into effect would be to contravene the democratic ideal.

But if democracy has no hierarchy of values—indeed, no preferred values at all—and if democracy does not suggest the specific attitudes an individual ought to adopt, the beliefs he ought to hold, and the particular body of facts he ought to "know", then the problem of teaching becomes an exceedingly intricate one, and the problem of teacher preparation is even more complex.[42]

Democracy and authoritarianism alike place upon teachers the obligation of modifying the beliefs, habits, attitudes and values of students. Authoritarianism can state quite clearly the specific changes it is trying to bring about. Democracy has no such specific wares to sell; for this reason many are inclined to accept operationally, even while they reject it verbally with some vigor, the proposition that the democratic ideal is bankrupt. If teachers are asked to bring about changes in pupils, and if they are forbidden to set up and work toward the specific changes they want to bring about, it would appear that we have laid upon them an utterly hopeless task.

It may help somewhat to repeat that the democratic ideal has been abstracted from a culture pattern—that we made it up as a meaning for activities which were going on within our experience. Widely divergent cultures may be characterized as "democratic" in several aspects, but it is quite impossible either to give specific content to "democracy" apart from a culture pattern, or to deduce the specific character of a culture from the word "democratic".

The apparent absence from the democratic ideal of distinctive and positive content is, however, only apparent. It results from a trick of language which has furnished footless entertainment to men of all generations. This is the trick involved in the formulation, "If a man says 'I lie,' and tells the truth, he lies; but if he says 'I lie,' and lies, he tells the truth." It is the trick which provides the quality of apparent self-contradiction that characterizes all possible answers to the ancient question, "Is the class of all classes that are not members of themselves a member of itself?"

We need to realize that whenever a word such as, "true," "false," "know," "believe," "value," (as a verb) and the like is used, our language has moved to one level beyond that in which we express whatever is "known," "believed," "valued," or held to be "true" or "false". The man who says "I lie" cannot possibly refer to the words he is then uttering; he refers to some formulation at a lower level of abstraction, if he refers to anything.[43]

The picture of authoritarianism asserting boldly "Here are my specific, preferred values that men can live by. Where are yours?" and of Democracy piping plaintively, like Simple Simon, "Indeed, I haven't any," is exactly such a trick. A more accurate response would be, "Democracy has no specific values *at the level of intellectualization at which all authoritarianisms operate.*"

When we have said that democracy has no preferred values, no orthodox beliefs, no official creed, we have correctly stated the case at one level of language—the level from which authoritarianism derives its sanctions and above which authoritarianism never goes, and dares not go. That is to say, authoritarianism can never stand off and examine or appraise the content of an accepted hierarchy of values, because it has nowhere to stand. The specific values *are* the frame of reference, and to move out of it, even for a peek, is to smash it.

But democracy can and does permit the intellectualization of its own position—indeed, democracy must insist upon that process in order to achieve a positive frame of reference at all. So long as democracy is held at the same language level at which authoritarianism asserts its values, the situation looks like a choice between a frame of reference with values and a frame of reference without values. No view of life could survive the acceptance of this latter status; a frame of reference devoid of positive values is no more than a blank sheet upon which each individual may write what he pleases.

This state of affairs is precisely what we ought to expect, so long as we remain at that level of abstraction which is the highest possible one for any authoritarian scheme. But a new level of language enables us to see the democratic refusal to espouse a hierarchy of preferred values as a positive insistence that values originate out of human experience, that standards arise through the common experiences of people living and working and thinking together, and that authoritarianism is simply the arresting of the process through which values and standards are generated. Authoritarianisms stop the process at different points and in different ways, but in every case they either deny that the process ever went on, or insist that it has now permanently ceased to operate. The values and standards upon which they fix are claimed as timeless and eternal, or as created somewhere outside the world of use and wont and imposed by a Supreme Being or a universal force.

In this sense, then, democracy asserts positive and definite values, which escape being called "preferred" only because at the level of intellectualization where democracy takes on its specific content there are no competing values over which the democratic values can be preferred. When democracy moves to a point of vantage for judging the ways in which values and standards originate and are maintained, authoritarianism can only call from its lower level, "You have no business to go up there!"

In a sense, therefore, it is quite unrealistic to talk about enabling an individual to "choose between" democracy and authoritarianism, as if these ways of life stood side by side. What we do, rather, is to help an individual to lift himself, at least momentarily, above the particular tradition out of which he has developed, and to let him see how his own and other sets of fixed standards have arisen in experience. As soon as he has stood inside the democratic frame of reference long enough to become conscious of its nature and of the commitments it involves, he is ready for the choice, "At which level do I propose to live the rest of my life?"

The man who has never faced this question can still participate in democratic living, but he cannot deliberately and purposefully make the democratic ideal his guide. In cases of conflict between groups, we easily lose him; he can, without consciousness of iniquity, ascribe final validity to his group's values of the moment, and join with others to hold those values as absolute. He is not committed to the widening of the group and the steady extension of common concerns as the method of democracy.

Nor is there any way of "indoctrinating" him in the democratic ideal. Indoctrination necessarily takes place at a level of intellectualization below the point where democracy takes on its specific and positive content. We could, indeed, indoctrinate *against* the values of any particular authoritarianism, but that would be to leave our victim at the mercy of the next plausible fixed system that came along. Commitment to the democratic ideal obviously involves much more than intellectualization, but it is quite impossible of achievement *apart from* intellectualization. The decision against indoctrination, within the democratic frame of reference, is therefore not a decision at all, but a recognition of what is possible. The reason why democracy cannot do business in that way is neither a sentimental squeamish-

ness nor a pusillanimous dread of violent action, but rather the simple fact that democracy has no offices on that particular floor.

A culture pattern at any moment, whether it tends in an authoritarian or a democratic direction, has and must have central and directing values of a fairly specific kind. Any authoritarian scheme sets forth clearly what these directing values must be. Democracy is concerned, not with the specific character of the directing values of the culture in which it is imbedded, but rather with the way in which central values come into being and are maintained or modified.

It is necessary to recognize, at the outset, that, *so far as any single individual is concerned*, the earliest acts of prizing or valuing grow out of and are built upon sheer animal preference. The human infant feels pleasure and pain, so far as we can tell, in about the same way as any other animal. Pleasure and pain get into his experience long before the process of carving objects out of his experience and identifying them has made any headway.

It must likewise be admitted that no method is known for purposely giving a particular direction to the behavior of little children except the method of conditioning, and that the development of certain personal and social habits which are indispensable both to the comfort and safety of the child and to the well-being of those who have to live with him can come about only because and insofar as the child's environment rewards the adoption of these habits and penalizes variations from them.

In the same way, the earliest beliefs of children are necessarily taken on, quite uncritically, out of the narrow environment that closely envelops little children in any society, democratic or authoritarian. Indeed, it is probably safe to say that, although the flavor of the relationships among adults in a democratic home may be sensed by a child long before he is capable of reflection, and although the very intent to develop self-direction in the child may strongly influence the precise methods employed by adults in conditioning him, the distinction between authoritarianism and democracy inside the experience of very young children will be at best an extremely subtle one.

A sharp practical distinction between authoritarianism and democracy as principles of social organization arises over the question, "Upon what shall we rely to secure that degree of agreement, both with regard to central values and with regard to fundamental beliefs, which all complex societies require in order to maintain themselves?"

The authoritarian answer is very clear. Authoritarianism relies upon the suppression or minimizing of *occasions for doubt*. As a consequence, the specific content of the beliefs and values taken on uncritically in infancy becomes a highly important matter. Uniformity among all the children in the state with respect to these beliefs and values, as well as consistency between them and the central values and preferred beliefs of the whole culture, is necessary if doubt is to be fully eliminated.

Equally necessary to authoritarianism is the creation of a climate of ideas in which expressions of doubt about fundamental beliefs or rejection of approved values are socially unacceptable forms of behavior. People must be taught to wear ignorance like a medal, and to say proudly, "I assure you I know nothing about such matters," or "Really, I prefer not to think about things of that kind." Steel whips and concentration camps are not the basis of authoritarianism, but only an exceptionally unpleasant consequence of it. The basis is the reliance by leaders, teachers, parents, or other authorities upon ignorance as a guide to the conduct of followers, pupils, or children. Social coherence and unity are guaranteed by (1) instilling preferred values and beliefs, (2) holding these values and beliefs as above or beyond question, and (3) carefully keeping out of people's experience any knowledge which might be seen as casting doubt upon the soundness of any preferred belief.

The foregoing paragraphs are not intended to suggest that authoritarian leaders have an easy time of it. Men think as naturally as they breathe, when occasions arise; and no one can wholly eliminate occasions for thinking from the experience of any individual. Even the process of minimizing such is beset with difficulties; but it will, after a fashion, do the job. It will unify and order nearly all the activities of nearly all the people in a state, giving them in some degree a sense of belonging, of commitment, even of security.

Democracies need these things quite as much as authoritarian societies need them. But democratic societies could in one emphasis be defined as societies which have found reliance upon the deliberately cultivated ignorance of the common man, as a method of social control, increasingly distasteful. In America, as we have seen in Chapter III, the areas which are held as above or beyond examination have dwindled to a very small number, and even these tend to open up whenever they limit practical action. Even beliefs about economics, religion, sex, and race, so far as these beliefs actually direct conduct, are not entirely protected from scrutiny. And certainly, although many would wish it otherwise, there is at present no carefully guarded core of uniform and consistent convictions around which our culture is built.

Upon what, then, may democracy rely for that degree of agreement which is indispensable to stability? How can men act together except in terms of common commitment to common convictions? And how can men hold to common convictions if they refuse to regard at least a few basic beliefs as settled, and to withhold them from critical examination? Can a man be fully loyal to that which he doubts, however slightly? Many a man has given his life under the banner "That the truth may prevail"; can men be expected to die for the slogan, "That the somewhat-more-probable may be preferred over the rather-less-likely"?

To the question "Upon what does democracy rely for securing a sufficient uniformity of belief to permit common action to go forward?" this writer proposes the reply, "Upon knowledge." The answers to the other questions in the foregoing paragraph depend upon an elaboration of this point.

As a precautionary measure, it would be well to disclaim at the outset the notion that men in a democracy acquire most of their beliefs through the process of examining the evidence for them. Nothing could be less realistic. We need to act far too quickly and far too often for that.

When the taxi pulls up in front of my house, I do not run over in my mind the evidence for my belief that the man operating it is in fact an employee of the cab company and a reasonably normal citizen. As a confirmed reader of mystery novels, I am not unacquainted with the remote possibility that the cab has been stolen by a homicidal maniac who is now systematically following up the driver's call-list. But this possibility never occurs to me as I step confidently into the cab; I accept the belief that this man is the regularly assigned cab-driver simply because I have no reason for doubting it. If I insist upon trying to marshal evidence in support of every belief in the light of which I act, I shall almost certainly be spotted within a day or two as a hopeless neurotic.

In one sense, of course, this illustration is unrealistic, because I do not in fact formulate any belief about the cab-driver at all; I just get into the cab. But this is true of all behavior in which no elements of doubt are involved; we simply "take in" the situation at the level of recognition, so that there is no need even to formulate beliefs about it, let alone to examine them.

The very concept of "evidence for", or affirmative evidence, is ordinarily forensic rather than psychological. The evidence *for* any proposition, as marshalled by a debater or a lawyer, is simply a reorganization, for purposes of persuasion, of the range of experience which the proposition seems adequately to take into account. Only when beliefs are held consciously as

hypotheses does affirmative evidence actually appear inside the reflective process. The process of inference may perhaps be regarded as a sudden identification of certain factors in a situation as "evidence for" the proposition inferred, but if so, its evidential quality is momentary and (in the form in which it is perceived) incommunicable. What we rely on is rather the *absence of negative evidence*, an absence which becomes steadily more significant as we extend the range of experience against which a given belief is tested. We can, and indeed must, accept out of the culture, without rigorous examination, an enormous number of beliefs for use in action; and so long as they are not controverted by some sort of negative evidence, we hold on to them. In this respect democracies and totalitarian states are alike.

Many men have reacted to the fact that we take on beliefs quite uncritically by protesting that we ought to do otherwise. Trotter, for example, writes:

> If we feared the entertaining of an unverifiable opinion with the warmth with which we fear using the wrong implement at the dinner table....then the dangers of man's suggestibility would be turned into advantages.[44]

James Harvey Robinson is of a like opinion:

> *We very rarely consider, however, the process by which we gained our convictions.* If we did so, we could hardly fail to see that there was usually little ground for our confidence in them. Here and there, in this department of knowledge or that, some one of us might make a fair claim to have taken some trouble to get correct ideas of, let us say, the situation in Russia, the sources of our food supply, the origin of the Constitution, the revision of the tariff, the policy of the Holy Roman Apostolic Church, modern business organization, trade unions, birth control, socialism, the League of Nations, the excess-profits tax, preparedness, advertising in its social bear-

ings; but only a very exceptional person would be entitled to opinions on all of even these few matters. And yet most of us have opinions on all these, and on many other questions of equal importance, of which we may know even less. We feel compelled, as self-respecting persons, to take sides when they come up for discussion.[45]

It seems to the present writer that the two demands implied in the foregoing quotations, namely, (1) that men shall refuse to accept beliefs unless they have been "verified", and (2) that they shall abandon all claim to opinions on matters they have not carefully investigated, is an unreasonable and paralyzing demand.

Anyone who sets about the business of "considering the process by which he gained his convictions" is certain to discover that most of them have simply been picked up willy-nilly, in what Robinson calls a "careless and humiliating manner."[46] The effect of this discovery, especially if the discoverer regards it as "humiliating", is one of profound shock. This might be wholesome enough, if it were not for the fact that the person thus suddenly persuaded of his own complete inadequacy may fail to recognize his own situation as the common condition of all mankind.

There is no more reason for being ashamed of sharing with everyone else the common, non-reflective origin of our earliest convictions than there is for being ashamed of the circumstances which have invariably surrounded conception or birth. We accept beliefs uncritically because as children we can do nothing else. Apart from the process of wallowing in a culture and picking up what they can from it, children cannot arrive at the point where reflection is possible. To demand the privilege of choosing our earliest beliefs reflectively is no more practical than insisting on our rights to have some choice about our ancestry.

The distinction between democracy and authoritarianism lies neither in the specific content of the beliefs taken on from the culture in

childhood, nor in the fact that they are accepted without examination, but rather in the degree and quality of the reliance which the society in question places upon them. An authoritarian society will be intensely concerned that these beliefs shall be the "correct" ones, because it rests its hope for stability and security upon insuring the uniform specific content of many of the beliefs of its members.

In the United States, we tend to concern ourselves much less about the specific content of a child's initial beliefs than about his ability to modify these beliefs appropriately later on. I am not here referring to the attitude of any parent toward his own youngster, because a great majority of parents assuredly do adopt an authoritarian reliance upon fixing very firmly, and, so far as intent is concerned, for life, the child's "right" initial beliefs, especially in the ticklish areas of religion and so-called moral standards. I refer rather to the attitude of the American public toward American children in general. No devout Lutheran would care to see his child brought up as a Roman Catholic, or a Unitarian, or a Baptist, but he is not ordinarily disturbed about the fact that millions of children in America are so brought up. The concept of heresy as a high crime, of "incorrect" belief as worthy of the death penalty, is an exclusively authoritarian concept.

It is in this sense that democracy places its final reliance for securing commitment to common goals upon common knowledge, and upon the development in each individual of the capacity for generating knowledge out of his experience.

Men may easily become impatient of the so-called "cultural lag"—that unhappy state of affairs in which the mass of the population continues to lend its support to the maintenance of social arrangements which, in the light of the knowledge that has been built up within the experience of experts, are palpably inadequate for modern conditions. But we cannot ask men who are full participants in a democratic society to direct their judgments in terms of knowledge they do not possess. To say that "sufficient knowledge exists" to justify sweeping changes in our social order makes very little sense if we mean by it only that a handful of men control that kind of knowledge.

So far as the ordinary man is concerned, the "knowledge acquired by experts" is simply another statement which claims to be authoritative and asks his support. He is bombarded by such claims and requests from all sides. Other things being equal, he is likely to prefer the beliefs he has already accepted without examination to new beliefs which he is in no better position to examine. In this preference he is clearly justified.

The development of people who are capable of steadily modifying their beliefs in terms of their adequacy for explaining a steadily wider range of experience depends upon two things: (1) improving and refining the reflective capacities of our population, and (2) breaking through the hard shell of traditional sanctity which encrusts many deeply rooted and emotionally charged beliefs. Whether these two jobs can be adequately done anywhere is a real question, testing more sharply than did the events of Lincoln's day whether any nation conceived in liberty and dedicated to the proposition that all men are created equal can long endure. The task has become in a real sense a race against time, and no man can wholly predict its outcome. One thing, however, is certain: the public schools are strategically the best-placed agency for getting the job done, and there is no time to lose. We have compromised and temporized too long, with the result that in the face of desperate crisis we are forced to waste valuable time and weaken morals in order to effect new compromises with the absolute authoritarian values we have tolerated and often fostered. This time the chips are down; the issue between democracy and authoritarianism is more clearly posed than it has ever been. To believe in democracy "with certain reservations", or "in due time", or "as an ideal, but of course it's impractical to act on it" is no

longer a tenable position, if indeed it ever was.

Because teachers are people, they too have soaked up out of the culture certain unexamined beliefs and values which they sometimes hesitate to expose to critical examination, even by themselves. Under any decent conception of teacher-training, these teachers have almost certainly had a chance, with some help, to stand off and realize that theirs are only some of the many sets of convictions which people have adopted without examination; that their own sets would assuredly have a different content if they had been born of another family or in a different locality; and that insistence on the validity of accidental and uncritical acceptance as a method for securing truth not only gives comfort to but actually justifies the Nazi ideology. They are, or should be, capable of realizing that whenever we hold any conviction in the light of which men act to be above or beyond examination, we urge the case for an irrational basis of conduct, for faith maintained by refusal to test, rather than by successful meeting of tests, and for deliberately cultivated ignorance as the method of preventing doubt. They have been, or should have been, led to face the question: "Is your fundamental loyalty to the democratic ideal, or to your own accidentally acquired habits?"

The foregoing paragraphs are in no sense an attack upon any specific belief which anyone may have happened to pick up. They urge simply that in a democracy all beliefs must be held on terms consistent with democracy—that they must be held as proper subjects for examination by the method upon which democracy places its basic reliance. The test of a belief is its capacity to explain and to organize human experience. Every belief must on demand[47] accept the role of hypothesis and prove its adequacy to explain and to order such relevant facts as may be adduced to test it. For example, anyone who asks his fellow-men to go on acting in the light of the belief that our economic system is self-regulating and can be trusted in times of peace to provide for the maximal welfare of all has the clear obligation to explain the events of 1929 in terms of his thesis.

The problem may now be summarized as follows: The ordinary high school student has accepted most of his beliefs uncritically, out of the culture. He could not have done otherwise. The inadequacy of his beliefs for enabling him to grapple effectively with the problems of today is appalling. Yet he has a "right" to his beliefs, in the sense that he cannot be expected to react to the injection into his experience of different possible beliefs by abandoning the old ones and taking on the new. From where he sits, the new beliefs differ from the old only by being less familiar—so far as their authoritarian character is concerned, they are identical.[48] We can communicate new beliefs to him only as ideas, or bits of purported knowledge. Unless he himself becomes able to carry forward effectively the process of "active, persistent, and careful consideration of a belief or supposed form of knowledge in the light of the grounds that support it and the further conclusions to which it tends,"[49] he and we are both helpless. And the carrying forward of this process requires that the student must locate within his own prior knowledge, or within such purported knowledge as he is able to dig up for the purpose at hand, the grounds on the basis of which belief may properly be vouchsafed to (or withheld from) any suggested proposition or idea.

It may be argued, quite correctly, that the "knowledge" which the child uses in testing a belief, whether it comes from his own prior experience or from research undertaken *ad hoc*, is still only "purported knowledge" and needs to be tested in its turn. This argument is valid as against an attempt to secure absolute certainty; it places unshakable assurance at the far end of an infinite regress. But if our goal is steadily more adequate beliefs, rather than eternal verities, the argument has no force. The student who has located, as grounds for believing a purported form of knowledge, other purported knowledge which he regards as *rather less doubtful*, and who has successfully used the belief under examination to explain and organize the purported knowledge which he later takes as evidence for the belief, has thereby, so far forth, rendered, *both the belief under examination and the supposed knowledge used to test it* relatively more certain. They have been arranged into a framework of mutual support. All of human knowledge gets its title to that name from its membership in some such framework.

Knowledge, then, has a special role to play in a democracy. So has the reflective process, through which knowledge is created and reconstructed. For these reasons, that which is often (and at times somewhat slightingly) referred to as "information" has likewise a unique role in democratic life.

The complexity of modern culture makes it quite impossible for everyone to explore intimately and at first hand all of the institutions and agencies that affect his daily living. No one can hope to acquire extensive personal familiarity with more than a fraction of the matters with reference to which decisions have to be made—decisions in which he ought to participate to the extent of his ability. He is therefore compelled to use as evidence, within the reflective process, assertions of other men about matters of fact—assertions which he accepts as factual, but which may, of course, whenever it seems necessary, be examined on their own account.

All sorts of valid charges may be leveled at history text-books and reference books; it cannot be denied, however, that they are loaded with potential information.[50] The word "information" and especially the expression "functional information" have been a source of confusion to educational thinking because of certain kinds of vagueness and ambiguity which the following chapter will seek to clarify. The point of the present chapter has been made if the special role of information in a democracy is seen to consist in its use within the reflective process for the purpose of testing the adequacy of the beliefs in the light of which men live.

V
THE ROLE OF INFORMATION IN THE LEARNING PROCESS

The word "information" is ordinarily employed in two somewhat different senses. We speak of information as that which enables one who is already in action toward a clear goal to carry on without the need to stop and think; and we also speak of information as any body of alleged facts considered as a possible source of evidence.

Except in regard to education, most of us are able to keep these meanings straight. The clerk at the information desk says, "Yes, sir? What can I do for you?" He would be affronted, and rightly, if we were to reply, "Your sign says 'Information'. Let's have some." He has a right to assume that the sign on the desk will be taken to refer to the kind of information that will immediately lead into the continuation of a previously initiated course of action, rather than to the *potential* information that sometimes causes us to call a book or a lecture "informing".

This difference in immediacy of use has led many people to call that which we demand from the clerk at the desk "functional information". This term is meant to be one of high praise. The schools are alleged to need much more of it in their curricula, and teachers point proudly to the ways in which youngsters can "put into practice," now and later, the "information" they acquire in particular courses. The familiar content of courses offered by the "traditional" school is in contrast antiquated and quite useless.

There is some soundness and much plausibility in this point of view. Information that functions is obviously preferable to information that does not; indeed, there is no conceivable defense for the latter from any imaginable point of view.

It may be useful to elaborate further the distinction between information that can be put to immediate practical use and such alleged information as, "Alexander crossed the Hellespont with thirty-five thousand troops and thus began a series of conquests that soon brought the whole of Darius' empire under his sway." A boy who knows the location of the telegraph office, and the different possible types of message, along with relative costs, relative speed of delivery, and number of words permitted at the base rate is able whenever necessary—and it is almost sure to *be* necessary, or at least desirable, fairly soon and increasingly often—to be intelligent about sending a wire. The boy who knows how many men Alexander had at the battle of the Granicus cannot at this late date do much about it.

In spite of the apparent reasonableness of the foregoing argument, the present writer is convinced that "functional information" about the telegraph office may be a trivial and puttering sort of business, while the fact that Alexander began his invasion with thirty-five thousand troops may well have a tremendous significance for the youngsters of today's world.[51] The question in either case is not one of any particular virtue in the specific content, but of whether the student makes reflective use of that content.

What is called "functional information" is very often so treated or regarded as not to be "information" in the reflective sense at all. "Information" in this latter sense gets its distinctive character from the fact that it plays, within some individual's experience, the role of *needed evidence*. The Latin idiom for "inform", *certior facere*, emphasizes the evidential character of "information"; "to make (someone) more certain" is precisely the function of the informing process.

One can easily put "pattern of action" information into a context that at first glance resembles reflection. It looks plausible to say that one who wants to see a particular play finds his action blocked because he does not know at what theater the play of his choice is running, and that he therefore turns to an appropriate page of his newspaper for "information" that will relieve his perplexity. Yet a moment's consideration will reveal that he never had any doubt worthy of the name "perplexity", and that his action was never seriously blocked. He knew how to proceed continuously on the basis of sheer habit, with scarcely a moment's hesitation. The name of the theater was needed, not as evidence, but simply as part of a pattern of action; and our man already knew exactly what to do in order to find it.

Where doubt and perplexity scarcely enter, where overt action goes forward almost uninterruptedly in terms of familiar habit-patterns, evidence has very little to do. We are able to deal with the situation at the level of recognition and to apply, without reflection, or with only the veriest trace of reflection, a ready-made pattern of action which will get us out of our difficulty.

It is for such a pattern that we seek when we ask a stranger, "How do I get to the Art Museum from here?" or when we check the spelling of a word in the dictionary. What this sort of so-called information has some slight evidential flavor is clear; that it is a far cry from the more complex uses of evidence in reflection is equally clear. One who seeks simply a ready-made course of action ordinarily does not desire, or in any significant degree get, information in its evidential sense.

The line between a request for information in its evidential sense and a request for a pattern of action is by no means sharp. The word "information" must probably continue to cover both, in deference not only to the continuity of one with the other, but also to common usage. But in that case we need to keep two *kinds* of functional information clearly in mind, even though in some situations it will be difficult to draw the sharp line that would enable us to classify our experience under one head rather than the other. If I ask you, "What is Jones' telephone number?" I will probably accept the response, "Randolph 7943," as a mere pattern of action to be dialed on the spot. But this acceptance is not *totally* blind, nor is your response utterly devoid of evidential bearing. If you were to tell me that the number is "Rumpelstiltskin 17,000,000" I would surely not act upon your statement. Or if, having dialed your suggested number, I am greeted by an unfamiliar voice, I may at once ask "Is this Randolph 7943?" In this case I am asking for information in its evidential sense. The response, "No, it isn't," serves to ground (so far forth) my belief that I have been correctly informed as to the number. The response, "Yes, it is" shakes that belief, and may impel me either to inquire further ("Is this John W. Jones' residence?"), or to check the number over again in the telephone book or with "Information", depending upon whether I can easily believe in the possibility of a strange voice answering Jones' telephone.

In general, however, it may be said that information, in its evidential sense, is sought in the process of planning the character of a delayed response. The question "What is Smith's address?" asked with intent to inscribe the response forthwith upon the envelope of a letter, is clearly a request for a pattern-of-action rather than for evidence. But the "same" question could be asked in the process of deciding upon the make-up of a committee whose members must, among other things, live close enough to each other to be able to meet frequently without serious inconvenience. In this case, "Smith's address" becomes critical evidence on the question "Will the addition of Smith's name to the present list retain in sufficient degree the quality of geographical proximity to one another which the membership of this committee must have?"

Information, then, functions either (1) to provide (for one who is already in action toward a clearly recognized goal) a ready-made pattern or program of action, or (2) to assist someone toward making more adequate a belief in the light of which he is now acting, or proposes to act, or frequently acts.

A great deal of confusion has grown out of the failure clearly to distinguish these two possible meanings of information-in-use. The possibility that information of the pattern-of-action kind may almost literally *tell* the learner-seeking-to-act what to do has given to that kind of information an air of usefulness which sets it off from other kinds of content. We are learning to ask of any purported "information", "How can a youngster *use* this piece of knowledge?"

One interpretation of this question, used as a test of what belongs in the curriculum, will eliminate all materials save those which consist *wholly* of the "pattern-of-action" kind of information (where and how to turn in a fire-alarm, where the nearest hospital is located, the mechanics of marking a ballot, how to judge textiles, and so on indefinitely). Probably we could assemble a long list of patterns of action which everyone can conceivably turn to good advantage in the every-day transactions of living. It is hardly possible, however, to accept this sort of pattern-of-action information as the only kind operating in the student's life, and to hold that *no information not of this precise character* is of any functional use.

Under another interpretation, the question, "How can a youngster *use* this piece of knowledge?" may mean, "On what matters significant to the youngster does this knowledge bear?" Of course, the question is still a fair and reasonable one, provided that those who ask it will stay for the answer.

If one accepts the view that all functional information is of the "pattern-of-action" kind, then history, almost alone of school subjects, stands exposed as altogether useless in our modern world. The English teacher can point out that "almost every child will have occasion to write some business letters." The teacher of mathematics can point to such activities as making change or keeping accounts or any number of activities involving computations of various sorts. Geography can function as children plan trips. Industrial arts and home economics are quite obviously within the pale.

History, on the other hand, comes close to being utterly devoid of information which can serve *per se* as a pattern-of-action. A theory of the role of historical information in the learning process must therefore begin by offering an alternative to the view that functional information must provide a clear, ready-made pattern-of-action.

Functional information of the pattern-of-action kind *becomes* functional by virtue of a pre-existing relationship between the person who is to use it and his environment. The person who seeks or demands this kind of information is already in action, and already envisages clearly the state of affairs he wants to bring about. The frequency with which one finds himself in a situation of this character accounts for the existence of reference books, information booths, dictionaries, classified advertising, directories, card catalogues, and dozens of other devices for giving men access to functional information when and as they want it. It is safe to say that every child, by the time he is ten, has had occasion to make use of such devices, or to call upon someone else to use them in his behalf. They are a part of the system of intentional signs which we have created in order to prevent certain kinds of problems from arising. Like the route numbers on a well-marked road, they guide us very effectively and inform us only occasionally.

Information in its evidential role, however, enters not only into the achieving of ends, but into the formulation or selection of ends-to-be-sought and into the reconstruction of the person who seeks them. It is to this process that the teacher of history must look both for his role and for his sanction. History must make its case for inclusion in the curriculum in terms of the potential significance of its content within the act of reflective thinking.

We have seen in Chapter IV that educational psychologists have tended to emphasize perceptual-motor learning rather than conceptual learning. By perceptual-motor learning is here meant that type of learning in which overt or implicit motor response to immediately present stimuli predominates. There is of course no sharp line between this kind of learning and the more complex ideational, or conceptual, or meaningful learning, so far as the student is concerned; but there is often such a line with respect to what the teacher intends. Moreover, even though it is probable that no learning carried on by secondary school students ever fails to involve both aspects in some degree, the validity of the distinction is attested by the fact that motor-perceptual learning is common among animals for whom conceptual learning is demonstrably impossible.

Motor-perceptual learning, or sheer "learning to", can, at any rate, be so clearly dominant in a given human learning situation that its ideational aspects can be located and defined only with difficulty. We say that a child learns to walk or to swim or to ride a bicycle, without intending to refer to anything that would ordinarily be called ideational learning.[52] After all, educational psychology uses the word "learn" primarily as a means of differentiating "learned" responses from responses due to instinct or to sheer maturation. In this sense, learning is the modification of behavior; so that all learning, as observed, shows itself as "learning *to*" rather than "learning *that*." The organism, by reacting, becomes the kind of organism that tends to react in certain habitual ways. A child who cannot swim learns by swimming and thus makes himself over into a child who *can* swim. He learns to do by doing.

To phrase the matter somewhat more conventionally, "learning", in this sense, means "the acquisition of a habit"; and, although for people it ordinarily involves some degree of conceptual learning as well, it is nevertheless characteristic of the behavior of rats or angle-worms as well as of human beings.

The formulation "we learn by doing" suggests by its very phrasing that it was designed to supply a needed corrective for the practice of rote memorization in the schools—itself, interestingly enough, a kind of "doing". Like all such formulations, it is subject to serious misinterpretation. In a great many quarters, the proposition "we learn by doing" has been so interpreted that its corollary reads "insure doing, and learning will take care of itself." This corollary often effectively relegates the idea of "learning *that*" to the status of accident, and renders information not merely unimportant, but often, if we take the formulation literally, inconceivable.

The present writer, however, finds the tendency to attack "progressive education" for an over-emphasis upon motor-perceptual learning somewhat anomalous. Whatever contrasts we may draw between "progressive" and "traditional" education, they have one thing (at the very least!) in common, namely, a tendency to make motor-perceptual learning the major business of each student. It is true that traditional schools professed to emphasize "subject-matter", or the potential content of reflective thinking; but this profession was seldom fulfilled in practice. The student learned to say things, and to write things, which would serve his purposes; in a sense, his problem was often one of how to condition the responses of his teacher in such a way that the sight of a particular name on a grade-card would elicit the response of inscribing an "A" or "B". The process was reflective, of course, but what was actually learned (e.g., that Mr. Smith takes off for guessing, or that Mr. Jones is a sucker for a lot of citations, or that Miss Brown likes to have you argue with her) was limited in application because narrow in range. Moreover, teachers so often told students what they wanted and expected that genuine problems arose only occasionally. Students in the traditional school learned to "do", and "learned by doing"; it may be fairly said, however, that they generally learned little enough about anything, and very little of what they were intended or supposed to learn.

Within the so-called "content" subjects, it is possible to carry on a kind of motor-perceptual learning which in many respects may counterfeit the mastery of subject-matter. Students may learn, for example, *to say* that Jefferson was responsible for the Louisiana purchase, and *to answer* the question "Who was responsible for extending the possessions of the United States in 1803?" by the name "Jefferson". If the question is ever raised in after-dinner conversation, or if a cross-word puzzle calls for a nine-letter word meaning "Brought about the Louisiana purchase", the student will be able to emit the "right" response; moreover, the student will be able to laugh heartily at anyone who, in a similar situation, makes any other response. This will probably be true even if the alternative response is the equally appropriate and perhaps more accurate nine-letter word "Bonaparte". The student thus "learns by doing" to do those tricks which many people have come to accept as evidence that one has been educated.

There is a world of difference, however, between learning *to say* that Jefferson brought the Louisiana territory and actually learning *that* he did so. The distinguishing characteristic of the human animal is precisely the ability to "learn that" rather than merely to "learn to". A parrot may learn *to say*, "Jefferson bought Louisiana", but no parrot can conceivably learn *that* anything of the sort is true.

Learning of a distinctively human character involves "acceptance for use in action"[53] of a statement or implied statement which the learner has hit upon as a *meaning* for some objects of experience, and which has the potentiality of being true or false. The learner in this sense learns "something", and we ordinarily express this "something" as a substantive clause introduced by "that". But the substantive clause is not that which he learns.

Human beings are able to act in the light of those things which they believe. When a person accepts for use in action a statement of belief, so that he may thereafter act, in a variety of situations, in terms of the *meanings* he may find for that statement, he has learned in a distinctively human sense. Acceptance for use in action involves something very different from the employment in speech or writing of a statement. It implies that one's confidence in the truth of the statement enters into and affects his subsequent behavior. He cannot, in this sense, "learn" that to which he is indifferent. When he learns to say words which apparently point to matters about which he is not concerned, it is because someone has succeeded in making the saying of the words a matter of real importance for him. He is interested in being able to say them at appropriate points, and, even without any understanding of the matter under consideration, he may learn to do this successfully, so long as the clues for appropriateness are clearly set up and are external to the meanings of the formulations themselves—as they often are in final examinations, for example.

To illustrate what is here meant by "learning *that*", as opposed to "learning to", let us imagine a student who encountered, during the presidential campaign of 1940, the argument that President Roosevelt had frequently acted in ways that seemed to many men to go beyond his constitutional powers, and that for this reason he ought not to be re-elected. If such a student had reacted to the argument by point out, among other examples of the many occasions on which presidents have laid themselves open to a similar charge, Jefferson's purchase of Louisiana, he would have done something very different in character from simply saying, "Jefferson bought Louisiana". Whether his conclusion took the form, "This particular argument against Roosevelt's re-election is not valid", or the equally logical form, "Hereafter I shall look upon Jefferson as in this respect unworthy of the high office he held," would make no difference so far as the present discussion is concerned; the point is that this particular student would have furnished clear evidence of having learned *that* a given proposition had, in his judgment, the property of warranted assertability. We cannot say *when* he had learned it; perhaps both the proposition itself and the circumstances surrounding the act it sets forth were simply called up by "the dead heave of memory" and *learned* on the spot as their relation to a present problem became clear. The fact remains that in this situation the evidence of genuine learning in the strictly human sense would be fairly convincing.

Learning in this sense means "the establishment of meaning-relationships among one's experiences." We encounter a new "object", we search our experience for possible meanings of that object, we check and test our hunches until we have created a meaning-relationship that seems to "work", "fit", "belong". The new meaning-relationship is added to the stock of meanings against which suggested meanings for future "experienced objects" may be tested— we "accept it for use in action."

Learning of information is either an elaborate counterfeit, or it is one of the by-products of an inquiry, simple or involved, carried on by the student himself. A youngster in action finds himself in a situation whose meanings are not clear, either because the situation does not immediately suggest any appropriate way of acting or because it suggests two or more mutually exclusive habitual responses. Into a situation of this kind reflection has a chance of entering; for, while the youngster may simply overlook the indeterminate character of the situation and seize upon the first course of action that occurs to him, there is also a chance that he may attempt to figure out just what it is that is blocking his action, formulate hypothetically some ways out of his difficulty, elaborate in imagination the probable consequences of their adoption, and accept for use in action the hypothesis which he finally comes to see as the meaning of the situation. Clearly, this accepted hypothesis "has been learned" as soon as it is carried over into action; it has even given rise to a habit, in the sense that further situations which are recognized as being "of the same kind" can be dealt with at the level of

recognition. But along with this simultaneous "learning" of a new habit and a new belief goes also the learning of *those facts which have been accepted as evidential* in the resolution of the problem. These facts "belong to" the child because they are that in his experience for which the new belief and the new mode of action furnish an appropriate meaning. He can, if pressed, intellectualize at this point by reversing the process; he can defend his chosen course of action by showing its meaning-relationship to the experiences in which it is grounded.

The foregoing rough description of the reflective process, together with the attempt to distinguish between pattern-of-action information and information as evidence, has been an attempt to give content to the following statement of purpose:

The Function of the Teacher of History

The central aim of the school in America must be to promote democratic living; but in this respect the school is not unique. Every institution; every set of social arrangements must come to accept this same purpose and submit to this same test if democracy as a way of life is to flourish. The school has as its own special share in this common task the development of young people into individuals who can effectively participate in the continuous reconstruction of the social arrangements within which they live. Such individuals must be capable of standing off and examining the culture that has shaped them; this means that they must be capable of continuously reconstructing the beliefs, attitudes, and values which they have absorbed out of the culture.

Whenever other agencies fail to perform their appropriate functions, the school gets the additional, residual job of doing whatever may be necessary to the carrying forward of its central purpose; but the school recognizes these activities as accidental, probably temporary, and in any case not intended primarily to be educative.

Within this framework, no teacher can be wholly and exclusively the teacher of a particular subject. He must use whatever he knows, from whatever source it may have been derived, so long as it seems well calculated to carry forward the independent reconstruction, by students, of their own experience. Nevertheless, the teacher of history may properly be expected to have a control of historical materials by comparison with which his knowledge in other fields will ordinarily be limited and fortuitous.

The specialized job of the history teacher, then, is to bring appropriate historical materials, plus whatever else he knows, to bear upon the beliefs of young people, in such a way as to stimulate and to aid in carrying forward within the experience of each student the process of reflective thinking.

Any attempt to formulate the goals of a teacher in a single statement describing a single process is properly suspect. The obvious advantage of simplicity in such a formulation is no substitute for adequacy. In order to make the foregoing statement of purpose stand up, it will be necessary to show that the reflective examination by a student of his own beliefs and of beliefs which he is considering for acceptance will:

(1) have an impact upon his attitudes and values which may result in their modification in desirable directions;

(2) help to bring the student to grips with the central problems of his own culture;

(3) break the grip of tradition upon the mind of the child, so that tradition becomes his counsellor rather than his master;

(4) under appropriate direction, lead into a growing understanding of and commitment to the democratic ideal.

Theory cannot, of course, establish the foregoing points. Theory does enable us to assert that the soundness of the proposal which is central to this study, namely that the history teacher should focus upon the task of getting students to utilize the materials of history, and other materials, in the reflective examination of the students' own beliefs and ideas, depends upon whether it can be shown to secure in fact, as teachers become equipped to put the proposal into practice, the four outcomes claimed or predicted above. In advance of practice, all we can do is to show clearly how the process is *supposed* to work, in the interest of securing, over a period of years, an adequate and decisive trial for it.

Shifting the emphasis in the teaching of high school history toward the use of historical materials in reflection requires reorientation at several points. In the first place, we need to consider what the term "subject-matter" is going to mean within the new frame of reference.

It is clear enough that what used to be called "subject-matter", namely, the content of the text-book or course of study, has status within the theory we are considering only to the extent that it actually enters into the reflective experience of students. We may reasonably anticipate that much of it will never get inside the process at all. Presumably we shall have to regard "subject-matter" in its familiar sense as "potential subject-matter" within the reflective process, which may or may not be learned, depending upon its coming to be seen as relevant.

What will constitute the actual subject-matter with which they teacher will expect to work inside the reflective experience of the student? In the first place, there is the "experienced object" for which a meaning is being sought. Any part of their experience which students identify and mark off for investigation will in this sense be conceived as "subject-matter".

In the second place, there is the body of previous learnings to which the new object must be brought into meaning-relationship. The new "object" may call into question, and render (for the time) indeterminate, an indefinitely large number of previous learnings, which, along with their remembered supporting grounds if any, now revert to the status of "subject-matter" in the new learning activity.

In the third place, we may simply be unable to relate the new "object" to our previous learnings without the intervention of further experiences, whose character (in this relationship, and only there) may appropriately be called "mediating". For example, Einstein could not with assurance "fit" the observed motions of the planet Mercury (in this framework the "new object") into the pattern of learnings which he had organized in order (among other things) to take these movements into account, without the "mediating experience" of observing during an eclipse those phenomena which would be expected to result from the "bending of light in the neighborhood of the sun.

We have, therefore, what at first may look to be three kinds of "subject-matter". It should be observed, however, that (1) all three "varieties" have, or else acquire during the process of learning, a quality of being expressible in propositional form, and that (2) any "variety" may at any time assume the role previously held by one of the others. That is to say, while "subject-matter" of any sort assumes a particular function in any single act of learning, this function is not in any sense fixed, nor can we predict in advance of any reflective act the role which any particular subject-matter will perform.

We are therefore justified in giving the name "subject-matter" to any belief or purported knowledge which *enters into the process* of reflective thinking. We are *not* justified (and this point seems to me to be important) in insisting that subject-matter is under the necessity of having at some time played a *particular role* in reflection, namely, the role of "new object". That is to say, there is no reason why we cannot use in reflection formulations which we have accepted as "facts" without any personal examination of their experiential grounds. We accept them at the level of communication, either uncritically or because, trusting the authority who communicates them to us, we assume that

he can ground them in experience. After all, we regularly "take on" beliefs, from early childhood to death, without examination in the light of their *grounds*. We do, of course, give them a quick once-over to see whether they fit amicably into the convictions we already hold; then we say either "I can't believe it", or "I can easily believe it."

It may be that a failure to recognize the place in reflection of that which has been accepted without examination lies behind the charge, often leveled at the position which is being taken in this study, that it reduces intelligent behavior to a "coldly intellectual" business. The charge would be valid against a claim that all subject-matter *used in* reflection must have been *acquired through* reflection. It is obvious enough that such a claim is not merely unrealistic but absurd.

All children bring into the classroom with them a motley aggregation of beliefs, many of which antedate even the possibility of reflective activity on their part. They are not able to say where their beliefs came from, nor could they conceivably discriminate between beliefs with supporting ground and beliefs taken on heaven knows how from the culture in which they have developed. Yet it is precisely these beliefs which must be a part of the subject-matter of any learning activity of which the children themselves are to be a part.

When we hand these children a body of purported knowledge and say "take this on, too", we are often merely increasing the mass of *unlearned*, meaningless propositions to which students are exposed in all sorts of ways within our culture. The radio, the press, the church or Sunday-school, the cinema, the stage, parents, relatives, neighbors, friends, the corner grocer or druggist, are blasting "purported knowledge" at the youngsters. Under the traditional conception of subject-matter, all that the school offers them is "more of the same".

It may well be that the materials with which all of these competing agencies and individuals bombard children are not appropriate in educational terms. I am by no means suggesting that extra-school experience will always or necessarily furnish any large part of the subject-matter with which the school needs to operate. My point is simply that, whether we like it or not, the beliefs that have in fact developed within a student as the result of extra-school experiences must necessarily be involved as subject-matter in any learning experience the school may set up.

I should like to underscore the words "whether we like it or not." In a very real sense, the beliefs, attitudes and values which youngsters bring to school are the youngsters themselves. It is useless to ask that they leave these things behind when they come to school so as not to inconvenience the teacher; we could as well ask them to leave their legs at home and thus avoid getting wet feet. However messy, garbled, confused, illogical, or groundless the beliefs of students may be—and we have seen that under the pressure of modern techniques for disseminating knowledge they are likely to be all of these things—they are nevertheless a part of our subject-matter.

The very increase in the range of potential experience which has resulted in confusion and uncertainty for many young people has within itself enormous possibilities for the enrichment of human living, provided that young people can apply the method whereby confused, contradictory, or apparently unrelated experiences are ordered, arranged, and brought under control. That method, the method of "reflective thinking", has been described in general terms; and we have seen that to make reflective thinking central in the teaching of history will at once compel us to modify our conception of "subject-matter" so as to admit into that category any formulation in language to which the pupil attributes truth, as well as all material, from whatever source, which is utilized in testing the adequacy of a student's belief, and thus takes its place, for that student, among what may be called "the facts of the case".

The reduction of this theory of the teaching of history to terms of curriculum and classroom method is the business of the next chapter. For the present, it is enough to get the theory stated in general terms, and to show that one who acts upon the theory may reasonably anticipate the four outcomes listed earlier in the chapter: an impact upon attitudes and values as well as upon beliefs; a coming to grips on the part of the student with the major problems of present-day living; a freeing of the student from the authoritarian aspects of his own tradition and culture; and a growing commitment to the democratic ideal.

(1) *The Impact of Information upon Attitudes and Values*

The question of how information secured through the reflective examination of one's beliefs can affect his attitudes and values is a difficult one. It is far easier to establish the proposition that information cannot touch attitudes or values in any other way. However, the paramount importance of values and attitudes in democratic living renders any educational program indefensible which leaves them out of account. The question therefore becomes, "Can the teacher of history who focuses his attention sharply upon the task of keeping reflection going, continuously, within the experience of each student, reasonably expect desirable modifications of attitudes and values to result?" A negative answer to this question would thoroughly blast the theory of the teaching of history which is offered in this chapter, so far as its singleness of directing purpose is concerned. It is therefore worth while to take some pains in the definition and clarification of the terms "attitude" and "value", especially in relation to the term "belief".

The notion that words like "attitude", "value", and "belief" can be defined in such a way that they will denote or correspond to specific, limited "referents" in experience is at the very least an optimistic one. Definition of this sort is possible when the referent is a concrete object familiarly known long before definition is attempted or when we do *not* intend to refer our terms directly to experience. In geometry, for example, we can define a "circle" in a way that marks it off from every other possible form—but in so doing we recognize that such "circles" are not encountered in the world of use and wont. It is generally possible, in any universe of discourse, to refine our terms until they are mutually exclusive and easily manipulated in relation simply to one another; unhappily, upon reaching that point we often discover that we are no longer talking *about* anything.

For practical purposes it is generally quite enough to choose words that indicate correctly the use to which their "referent" is to be put; we may safely call the stuff that spurts from a drinking fountain "water", rather than "a weak solution of sewage and chlorine", because we propose to drink it, rather than to perform a chemical experiment with it.

In discussions of theory, however, it is often necessary to come at the meanings of words by treating them in pairs and discriminating between the members of each pair. So-called "polar" words, like "up" and "down", or "good" and "bad", or "static" and "dynamic" are only particular and obvious cases of the general proposition that the meanings of words which refer to experience are relative. To illustrate, we may get at the meaning of "work" by opposing it to "play"; in that case, all sorts of activities can be arbitrarily arranged along a linear continuum, according to the degree to which they seem (to the arranger) to approach one pole or the other. But if we choose as our polar words "work" and "drudgery", then the same elements in an activity which previously pushed it *away from* the "work" pole will now have exactly the opposite effect. To conclude from this fact that "there is no such thing as work" is utter nonsense if by the expression we mean "the word 'work' cannot of itself convey any sort of meaning." The point is simply that for certain purposes a single word will not convey *enough* of meaning with sufficient accuracy.

Since all three of the terms with which we are now concerned overlap in almost every actual situation, it seems wise to deal with them as the meanings of the continua "attitude-belief", "attitude-value", and "belief-value." All three terms could of course be treated in other connections, and their meanings would then be significantly different. If we were to set up "attitude-act" as a continuum, for example, our results would be of a very different character, and in certain situations (e.g., a discussion of what constitutes "assault" in common law) they might well be appropriate and useful. So might dozens of other pairings of the word "attitude". The discussion which follows is an attempt to get at those aspects of the meanings of "belief", "value", and "attitude" that seem relevant to the present problem of their inter-relationship, rather than to arrive at any exclusive definition of the terms.

If we apply the operational test of meaning to the word "attitude", we get something like this: "the meaning of 'attitude' depends upon the operations by which we determine and describe an attitude."

Accepting this test, it is possible to say that an "attitude", in the sense in which teachers can consider or deal with "attitudes" of students, is simply a generalization about the behavior of an individual. If Johnny meets all attempts at conversation with short, ungracious replies, if he rarely takes any part in group games or discussion, I may *make up* the generalization, "Johnny adopts an unsociable 'attitude'." If, on the other hand, Johnny gets along well with other youngsters and is unfriendly to teachers, janitors, visitors, nurses and librarians, I may speak of his "unsociable attitude toward adults"—a generalization which would need further modification upon the discovery that his relations with his parents, the basketball coach, and the store-keeper were quite satisfactory. It is not necessary to postulate any metaphysical entity *in* Johnny to which the name "attitude" refers—it *subsumes*, without in any detailed sense explaining, a wide range of fairly specific behaviors. More fully, then, under this definition, an "attitude" is attributed to an individual as an elliptical substitute for a generalization which purports to subsume a range of behaviors of that individual; it functions as a convenient tag or label for a working hypothesis to be used in dealing with the individual to whom the "attitude" is attributed. The hypothesis itself has of course a broader purpose than that of a mere label; it serves also to mark a *direction* for subsequent explanation, to make explicit and urgent the consciousness of need for such explanation, and to condition the evidential weight which may be attached to Johnny's behaviors in other contexts (e.g., the extent to which Johnny's unresponsiveness to his teacher ought to be allowed to suggest that the teacher lacks the capacity to secure rapport with young people).

An "attitude" in this sense need not involve reflection or even self-consciousness—it could with equal validity be imputed to persons or to animals. Whenever a variety of behaviors is found to characterize a single organism, it is possible to classify these behaviors into groups, and to label each group as an "attitude", baptising the attitude with some title derived from the meaning of the criteria in terms of which the "grouping" has been made.[54]

To deal directly with attitudes at this level is obviously impossible except by animal-training methods. In a democracy, education must approach "attitudes" of this kind indirectly, at the level of consciousness, since democracy has presumably no "orthodox" attitude to sell.[55]

It is important, therefore, to distinguish between those attitudes which "just happen" to belong to an individual (not in the sense that they are "uncaused", but in the sense that their possessor assigns no cause to them) and those attitudes which are adopted consciously (or come to be held consciously) as alleged implications of beliefs.[56] To illustrate, a white child may simply "take on" an unfriendly attitude toward Negroes. There will be environmental "reasons" for this

outcome, but the child will not be aware of them as reasons. We could perhaps bring about change by pulling him out of the culture in which his attitude has developed and planting him in an artificial environment designed to build into him another, and to some of us a more "acceptable" attitude—but insofar as he simply takes on the new one in the same way as the old, his attitude, even if reversed, remains qualitatively the same thing—an unexamined habit-complex taken on quite uncritically.

Fortunately, in describing other men's "attitudes" we have a source of evidence in addition to their behavior, which we regularly (if not always frankly) draw upon whenever we attempt to consider that behavior thoughtfully. In a sense, therefore, an attitude is not fully defined by a statement of specific operations through which we come to know it. A physical concept like "length" does indeed involve simply the "method of measurement", and to talk of "length" in any other sense is meaningless. But when we talk of other men's attitudes, we have a source of information in addition to the behavior of the men we are discussing. That source is the intellectualization of our own apparently comparable experience, and any attempt to leave it out of the picture does violence to the nature of the world we live in.

All of our human relationships are carried on in terms of the assumptions, first, that other men are in many respects a good deal like ourselves, and second, that we can somehow stand off and look at ourselves in such a way as to gain insight into the business of looking at others. If I were insensible to pain, my neighbor's anguish could never be communicated to me. I would be reduced to describing a man with a toothache somewhat like this: "He groans. He contorts his features. He writhes. I have observed that these behaviors often accompany one another, and that they are frequently found in conjunction with dental caries. I shall label the group 'Reaction Z (dental)' for convenience in notation."

Perhaps the safest statement we can make about "attitudes" is that they involve the emotions. How do we know this? Whether we like it or not, we can know of joy, fear, grief, love, only as we become conscious of ourselves. Jones's behavior with relation to antique furniture is understandable to Smith because Smith knows of an emotional experience which accompanies his own somewhat similar behavior toward rare postage stamps. Any statement regarding another man's attitude is certain to include, by virtue of the very language chosen, not merely a description of his behavior but also a guess as to the probable character of an assumed *emotional accompaniment* of that behavior; indeed, it is this guess which determines in the first instance the precise *selections* from the individual's total behavior which we decide to class together as indicating an attitude, and in the second, the character of the verbal label we place upon that selected behavior. The behavior of an actor on the stage is selected in terms of the emotion which the audience is expected to attribute to the character portrayed. In the same way, the behavior of a labor spy is deliberately chosen in terms of the attitudes which fellow-workers are expected to impute to him as among the reasons for his behavior. He may, for a time, seem to do all the things a good trade-unionist might do—the significant absent factor is the emotional reaction which, because of his supposed commitment to the union's purposes, might *normally be expected* to accompany such behavior. Without that factor, his behavior functions as a worthless check on the bank of his attitudes, beliefs, and values; if his fellow-workers accept it, they will eventually learn that there are no funds behind it.[57]

It is through intellectualization of our experience that we learn to ascribe an emotional basis or a motivation to the behavior of others. And it is to the same source that we must turn first when we attempt to discriminate between "attitudes" and "beliefs".

One distinction between "belief" and "attitude" may be drawn on the basis of self-con-sciousness: a belief must be an object of knowledge for the believer, a propositional formulation to which he attributes the quality of being *true*. An attitude, on the other hand, need not be conceptualized by its possessor. It is (as we observe it in others) simply a distinctive kind of habit-complex, characterized by the fact that we feel warranted in ascribing to it an emotional content of a particular character.

A second difference is that if we do formulate an attitude of our own in words, the subject of our statement is always and of necessity "I". Subject, of course, is used here in its logical rather than in its grammatical sense; an attitudinal statement like "Poetry makes me sick" predicates something about "me" which has a much more general significance than anything it says about "poetry". An attitude can only be stated as a relationship between the *self* and something in the environment. One end of the relationship is firmly rooted in the personality of the man who "has" the attitude.

A belief, on the other hand, may be expressed as a proposition neither of whose terms is "I" or "me".

For example, "I do not like Negroes" states an attitude. "Negroes are intellectually inferior to the white race" states a belief. The man who makes the first statement may indeed be misrepresenting himself, but there is a sense in which the truth of his assertion is for him alone to judge—it is not, except under unusual conditions, a reasonable matter for public inquiry. The second statement, on the other hand, can be dealt with reflectively, "in the light of the grounds that support it and the further conclusions to which it tends."

If the speaker has woven into his attitude the reasoning of some such writer as, say Lothrop Stoddard, and has conceptualized and rationalized it, his attitude has become a qualitatively different and distinctively human thing. I can teach a dog to bark at Negroes, but I cannot teach a dog to justify this conduct. At the level of consciousness, the attitude becomes implicated with a *belief*, that is to say, it becomes an attitude *consciously* held to whose justification can be expressed by its possessor as a proposition.

So long as an attitude remains below the level of consciousness, so that it must (to be known at all) be ascribed to an individual by *others*, rather than consciously held to by *himself*, there is no way under the sun in which subject-matter can be brought to bear upon it. And even when the attitude itself is known to its possessor, it may remain simply an attitude, unrelated to belief of any kind, and therefore inaccessible to subject-matter. The man who refers his aversion to Negroes to the proposition "Negroes are unintelligent", or "Negroes are irresponsible", can be met with subject-matter which is *evidential*—but the man who says flatly, "I just can't *stomach* them," and lets it go at that, can disregard all the Carvers and Robesons and Dunbars and Duboises and Andersons we may assemble. It is no good to ask him to be reasonable, because he does not even pretend that his attitude involves anything different from the aversion of a timber-wolf for fire or a moth for camphor.

I should not like to be understood in any of the foregoing paragraphs as arguing for a sharp separation between sheer visceral preference and attitudes based upon consciously held beliefs. It must be granted that a belief-structure built up to defend a pattern of emotional preferences does not in any sense *remove* the visceral basis upon which it was constructed, and that visceral responses are not automatically abolished when the beliefs which sanctioned them have been altered or broken down. I am urging simply that some attitudes lie wholly below the level of self-consciousness, that some attitudes are held consciously but involve only emotion, and that other attitudes involve both emotions and consciously held beliefs; and that among the many differences between these kinds of attitudes is the fact that the last named can interact with an unlimited quantity of subject-matter, while the first two represent closed, autonomous systems to which, so long as they remain unrationalized, no possible subject-matter is relevant in an evidential sense.

Fortunately, the fact that the individual has his being within and through a social milieu with which he must somehow come to terms generally impels him to rationalize his attitudes whenever they are seriously opposed. To rationalize an attitude is to make it respectable, in the sense that it is cast in the propositional form which makes it subject to testing. It becomes a part of the conceptual currency of society—it can be talked about, considered, thought of, evaluated, examined.

Whenever anyone puts into language a propositional statement of a belief, it is possible to cluster about his statement a quantity of evidential subject-matter which will make the belief in some sense *different*, even if the propositional statement remains unchanged, since a generalization depends for its quality upon the range of experience which it effectively subsumes. What happens to other beliefs after the individual has, as it were, taken the reconstructed belief "back into himself" is one possible measure of educational effectiveness.

If we assume that the propositional statement represents a genuine belief to which the student is fully committed and about which he *cares* deeply, it is safe to say that, as a result of its reconstruction, further significant change in the individual is likely to go forward. If, on the other hand, the statement of belief is given off-hand and is regarded as trivial by the student who offers it, the outcome may well be of no consequence. A lot of superficial sparring, in which nobody cares much about any of the points allegedly at "issue", goes on in the name of promoting reflective thinking.

To go further with this line of thought requires an attempt to deal with the question of "values", with the continua "value-attitude" and "value-belief", and with the relation of values to subject-matter.

For purposes of this discussion, "value" will be taken to mean "anything that is valued (prized, cherished) by anybody." The *act* of "valuing" is here conceived as the sole possible basis for the existence (as such) of the "thing valued." Thus "pleasant weather" could not be valued in a land where storms were unknown and a perfectly even climate prevailed, except by those who through some sort of experience had come to know that the local weather conditions were not universal. The act of valuing is in the first instance an act of discrimination, in which the "thing valued" is set off, as it were, against other things to which (severally, of course,) it may be regarded as in some respects polar. Men did not value "fresh air", or even think of air as "fresh", until they had developed conditions which produced "foul air." We do not list among the things we "prize" the facts of gravitation, unless we have imagined (in the more colorful vernacular "dreamed up") a state of affairs in which "gravitation" is not involved.

In the process of living, sometimes when in search of other values and sometimes driven by a sort of *vis a tergo* of which modern life offers many examples, we *come upon* things in our experience which we are able to conceptualize, enjoy, and "want more of." Purpose arises as we endeavor so to modify our living that we shall get more of that which we have come to value—and in carrying on purposeful activity we continue to stumble upon materials out of which we make values.

Nor are values always found by chance. We go to some pains, indeed, to find pegs upon which to hang our preferences. A great many familiar activities, such as window-shopping, travel, browsing in bookstores, or skimming a magazine article may be looked at as efforts to find the stuff from which to make values. This is true because most of us come fairly early to conceptualize "valuing", and to accept the "act of valuing" as itself a valued act.[58]

The interpenetration of the meanings of the terms "belief", "attitude", and "value" is of course very extensive. For example, an individual ordinarily values his beliefs highly. When, in any particular case, he does not, it is safe to say that the beliefs in question have been taken on casually and are lightly rooted. The prevalence of rationalization is sufficient warrant for saying that beliefs take a high place among any individual's values. Beliefs also involve, or are involved in, attitudes; they lead to attitudes; and they result in part from attitudes. Attitudes and values are inseparable if we allow the concept of "negative valuing"[59] and if we eliminate cases of compulsive behavior and other psychic derangements.

It is clear enough, then, that we need not be afraid of leaving values and attitudes untouched by focusing upon the reflective process, so long as we consider the beliefs students bring with them as a part of the subject-matter students are asked to order and arrange through reflection.

Whether the modifications of attitudes and values that may be anticipated within this process may be expected to take a desirable direction depends upon what we mean by "desirable". If we mean that we have in mind a set of values at which we want youngsters to arrive, or (which is the same thing) a set of attitudes toward specific matters which we want them to adopt, we cannot hope, except by accident, to achieve our goals through fostering reflective thinking. Once thinking starts, nobody knows what will happen to values and to attitudes. In Dewey's[60] words:

> Every thinker places some portion of an apparently stable universe in jeopardy, and no man may wholly predict what will emerge in its place.

All we can reasonably predict about the effect of the proposed approach upon values and attitudes is that there will almost certainly be an effect, and that it seems likely to be in the direction of making the student steadily more conscious of the values he holds and of their relationships to one another in a widening range of experiences.

(2) *Bringing the Student into Contact with Major Problems*

That the reflective examination by a student of his own beliefs and of the tradition out of which they have arisen will bring him sharply against "the quandaries of our life today" should be evident if we consider the sources from which unexamined beliefs are drawn. The apparently more direct approach of "presenting" modern problems, in the form in which statesmen, industrialists, labor leaders, social scientists, or educators face them, is often unsuccessful because the "problems" presented are not, in that form, accessible to the student. Except by accident, a presented problem is not *his* problem; rather his problem is to write a paper or take part in a panel discussion in such a way as to meet the requirements set up by the teacher. Such an approach may be very effective in eliciting statements of belief, toward which evidence may then be directed in such a way as to stimulate reflection and carry it forward; but unless this latter step is actually taken, the outcome is more often what has been called "the forensic display of ignorant opinion."

There is a sense in which virtually all of the problems of today's world grow out of the inadequacies of men's beliefs. In the presence of ample physical facilities for production and distribution of goods, men may sit shivering and hungry, while other men learn to look at them without compassion, for no better reason than that almost all of them have absorbed from the culture certain beliefs about the automatic working of the economic system, about the nature of ownership, about the appropriate function of government in human affairs, about human nature. Unexamined beliefs about the relationship of race to cultural possibilities may bring humiliation and suffering to one large section of our people, and callousness and arrogance to another.

The beliefs which have produced many of our major social problems are shared in varying degrees by the children who come to our schools. Few of them, indeed, could formulate the belief that our economic system works by automatic controls, and is best let alone to do its job. But many are sure that economic success is roughly proportionate to merit and industry; that what's good for business is good for the country; that those who work for the government are parasites and tax-eaters; that extension of governmental power, while a necessary evil in war time, is always to be deplored; that the statement "the poor ye have with ye always" ranges God on the side of those who shrug their shoulders at widespread poverty; that Negroes are naturally shiftless; that nobody would work without the fear of privation and poverty; that businessmen could not be expected to work without the incentive of profit; that any laborer who is not willing to work under almost any conditions, rather than remain "idle" (i.e., out of a job) deserves no consideration from society.

The location of the particular beliefs held by individual students in a given classroom is in the main a task to be performed on the spot. Some suggestions for procedure are given in Chapter VI. We are reasonably safe, however, in guessing that, whatever their specific form or content, the beliefs of young people in America, like those of their elders, follow closely the patterns of the tradition out of which our major social problems have developed.

(3) *Freeing the Student from the Grip of Tradition*

To assert that the reflective examination by the student of his own beliefs looks like a promising way of liberating him from a blind adherence to tradition is almost tautological. The only way in which tradition can bind or confine the intelligence of an individual is through his uncritical acceptance of traditional beliefs, attitudes and values. Since men have to grow up in a culture, and since no culture can operate without values and standards, the reflective examination of what we pick up out of the culture is the only alternative to a blind reliance upon tradition.

(4) *Securing Commitment to Democracy*

Commitment to the democratic ideal, so far as secondary school students are concerned, is ordinarily a matter of finding out what that ideal means. Obviously, the general atmosphere of a school, as the student senses it, will be of critical importance in the matter of getting into the student's experience the stuff out of which a concept of democracy may be created. However, he cannot get *enough* material in that way; he needs also to come at the nature of human relationships in his state, in his nation, and, for that matter, in the world. The history teacher who works in terms of the theory outlined in this chapter may therefore hope to strike several blows for democracy.

In the first place, his procedure requires him to welcome and to take seriously any opinion, conviction, or hypothesis that any student may assert. This single fact will go a long way toward making each student feel that he is a part of whatever is going on and to encourage extensive participation.

In the second place, a critical examination of beliefs which have in large part been accepted out of the tradition will almost certainly lead students toward the question, "What is the source of standards and values, anyway?" The pursuit of that question is one of the shorter roads to a clear distinction between authoritarianism and democracy.

In the third place, a steady emphasis upon the method of reflection seems likely to give some students an opportunity to conceptualize reflection itself, and to come to rely upon it as the exclusive method for determining truth. Such a reliance, as has been shown in Chapter III, is indispensable to purposefully democratic living.

On the whole, then, it would appear that the theory set forth in this chapter may be worth a try. In Chapter VI, an attempt will be made to indicate some of the meanings of the theory for curriculum and method in history.

VI
IMPLICATIONS FOR CURRICULUM AND METHOD

One of the persistent problems in translating the intent to promote reflection into terms of curriculum and method has been the tendency of teachers to identify "reflective thinking" with what has been called "the complete act of thought." This act is ordinarily described (with some variations of phrasing) as involving the following steps:

1. The occasion of reflection, which arises when our routine, habitual ways of behaving are interrupted in such a way as to create a doubtful or indeterminate situation.

2. The definition of the difficulty, or the identification of what it is that is blocking our action.

3. The rise of suggestions out of our prior experience, any one of which may or may not be adequate to dispose of our difficulty, remove the doubts that have arisen, and get us back into action.

4. The mental elaboration of suggestions, which involves their use as hypotheses to explain or take into account what we have observed as the facts of the case, and the prediction of things that would logically follow if the hypotheses are sound.

5. Testing, which involves the verification of our predictions and the judging of the adequacy of a suggested hypothesis to account for such new facts as we may come upon in the process of our inquiry.

6. Conclusion, or the actual moving back into action on the basis of a hypothesis which has satisfactorily met the foregoing tests.

Dewey[61] summarizes the complete act of thought briefly in five steps:

1. a felt difficulty,
2. its location and definition,
3. suggestion of possible solution,
4. development by reasoning of the bearings of the suggestion,
5. further observation and experiment leading to its acceptance or rejection; that is, the conclusion of belief or disbelief.

Educational philosophers differ in their ways of describing the complete act of thought, but the differences have to do largely with emphasis. Thus Bode is concerned that the testing aspects of the process shall stand out, while Kilpatrick focuses sharply upon the origins of problems. Aside from emphasis, however, the descriptions offered by these philosophers do not differ at all from Dewey's classic account.

All the efforts of these and other writers to point out that a complete act of thought, exactly as described, is probably a rare occurrence, that the order of the steps may be varied or the steps telescoped, that the purpose of the analysis is not to provide a prescription, but to indicate the significant aspects of thorough, painstaking reflection, have not served to keep teachers from identifying reflective thinking with the complete act of thought as analyzed above. Nor should this be wondered at. The appeal of a clear, step-by-step description to people who are products of our educational system is likely to be very strong. Such a description is "something we can get our teeth into," in terms with which we are familiar; it can be "grasped" as one "grasps" a listing of the steps by which a bill goes through Congress, or a summary of the provisions of the Peace of Utrecht—that is to say, it can be understood, illustrated by examples, and remembered.

As soon as the teacher turns toward the task of causing secondary school students to carry forward complete acts of thought, frustration sets in. The teacher knows that the pupil must start with a problem, but how shall that state of affairs be brought about? He knows also that problems will surely arise in each pupil's life; but these problems are hard to discover, often only vaguely formulated, and frequently of a character such that the subject-matter involved in them is beyond the possible reach of the teacher. In any case, the child whose action is blocked will often, after a brief sizing-up pause, leap impulsively into action in terms of the first hunch that occurs to him, and there goes his "problem". Or the problem may simply evaporate, as when Annabelle's desperate search for a method of winning back Henry's affection is abruptly halted by a date with George; or when a new puppy destroys Tommy's zeal for completing the birdhouse he has been building.

It is hard to disagree with Kilpatrick when he says that:

> In order for the life process to grow in the desired richness and fineness, this very process must and will make use of the cultural stores embodied in persons, in institutions, in books and other cultural works. The life process, to the degree that it is well directed from within, will call for the intelligent and sympathetic mastery and application by the pupils themselves of what is got from these cultural stores. When things are thus sought and used because a life situation inherently calls for them, they are better learned both because they are personally desired and because they are more intelligently thought through and used. These are ideal conditions for study and learning.[62]

One may, however, be pardoned for wondering what is supposed to be the antecedent of "these" in the concluding sentence. It is clear that a student who, within the "life process", encounters a situation which he can solve only by drawing upon the "cultural stores", is very favorably placed so far as getting the reflective process under way is concerned; indeed, if the situation "inherently calls for" these cultural stores, a teacher has little more to do than to make them available, so far as possible on demand.

But when a student with a problem of sufficient depth and significance to "call for the intelligent and sympathetic mastery and appreciation....of what is got from these cultural stores" is postulated as among the "ideal conditions" for study and learning, we get little help. It is as if we were to say that a large quantity of money, well invested, is an "ideal condition" for getting rich. Given the "condition" Kilpatrick postulates, his conception of a learning experience seems thoroughly sound:

(1) Suppose a child faces a situation. First of all there is in him that which makes this a situation for him, and second there is in the environment something that so stirs him that he is moved to act. Only as these things happen together does a child face an actual situation.

(2) Facing thus an actual life situation, the second step is to analyze it, partly to set up or clarify ends, partly to get materials for the planning that comes next.

(3) The third step is to make one or more plans and choose from among them, for dealing with the situation. In a developing situation the plan will be in process of making from step to step as the situation develops.

(4) Then comes the step of putting the plan into operation, watching meanwhile to see how it works, so that if need arise revision may be made.

(5) If the plan succeeds, a final stage is the backward look to see what has been done and how it might be done better another time.[63]

Inspection reveals at once the close parallel between Kilpatrick's "curriculum unit" and the analysis of the complete act of thought. Most teachers, however, are at a loss as to how to actualize the condition which Kilpatrick assumes, namely, that students can regularly locate and go to work on problems which are genuinely their own, and which are sufficiently clear and urgent to fix the end of thought and to sustain thought.

Kilpatrick appears to believe that children, unless "ill or miseducated,"[64] are just naturally capable of thorough, persistent reflection; but since virtually all children in secondary schools have obviously (by Kilpatrick's standards) been miseducated, in school and out, for many years, the practical utility of his formulation is not too clear. Whether the inner nature of students is such that they would be able to direct themselves reflectively if they had not been perverted and corrupted by "teachers who will not have it so"[65] is for our purposes academic; whatever the reasons, students in secondary schools do not regularly engage in the sort of planned, reflective pursuit of self-created goals that Kilpatrick takes for granted. The school's task is to *develop* that kind of behavior—if it were indeed the usual high school student's "natural" behavior, the need in a democratic society for a special agency like the school could well be carefully re-examined.

The sort of examination of a cherished belief which results from its holding, in the experience of a student, the role of hypothesis in a complete act of thought, is clearly desirable; for an individual thoroughly sophisticated in scientific method it is also, occasionally, possible. It depends, however, upon one's having conceptualized the reflective process and rigorously applied it on purpose. Moreover, even for the highly trained scientist, the belief to be tested will ordinarily be a new candidate for acceptance, rather than what might be called a charter member of his belief-patterns. Consider, for example, the tests of an adequate belief which nine members of the philosophy staff at Columbia University proposed in 1923:

1. *Clarity.* A good belief is unambiguous. We know unmistakably what it means.

2. *Consistency with the facts.* A good belief is founded on extensive and accurate observation. It is not contradicted by experience.

3. *Consistency with other beliefs.* There is a presumption against a belief that conflicts with other beliefs well certified by experience. Sometimes, however, it is the latter beliefs rather than the former that need to be revised.

4. *Utility.* A good belief is often distinguished by its usefulness in suggesting further good beliefs.

5. *Simplicity.* Other things being equal, that belief is best which makes fewest assumptions.[66]

The capacity to apply tests like these is a rare and magnificent achievement, even for presumably well-educated adults. The ability to turn such a powerful methodology back upon the kinds of beliefs men pick up in childhood and incorporate into themselves is surely a jewel without price, to be desired and cherished. But the writings of such distinguished scientists as Millikan, Eddington, or Jeans readily indicate that even those whose skill and insight in applying the methods described above are a source of admiring wonder to their contemporaries are nevertheless unable (some would say "unwilling", which in this context comes to the same thing) to apply scientific method to the consideration of their own naive and unexamined beliefs about such matters as religion, morality, and the origin of standards.

The teacher in the secondary school must be satisfied to stimulate and promote a much lower level of reflection than is described in the analysis of a complete act of thought. Indeed, he must be satisfied to inject *any* degree of reflection, at *any* level, into the ongoing experience of his students.

Reflection at its simplest level involves nothing more than the relationship of *significance*. That is to say, reflection implies that something is believed, or disbelieved, "Not on its own direct account, but through something else which stands as witness, evidence, proof, voucher, warrant; that is, as ground of belief."[67] We say that one thing "means" the other. This "pointing" quality, this relationship between a fact which is "known" (i.e., believed on its own direct account at the level of recognition) and a further fact which is suggested by it and believed for that reason, characterizes all reflection, from simple inference to the most elaborate scientific thinking.[68]

The irreducible elements of reflection (seen as the process by which the relationship of "pointing", or "meaning" is created) are two: a state of perplexity or doubt, and a search for facts which will reduce doubt (or induce belief, which is the same thing) in a degree sufficient to allow action to go forward. "Action" as here used need not refer to any large or complex task in process; it may refer to as simple a matter as attempting to express oneself clearly in an informal conversation. Anything that renders belief at all uncertain is a sufficient occasion for reflection.

A part of the teacher's task, then, is to create what could be called a problematic atmosphere— a set of conditions likely to render the beliefs of students in some degree doubtful. For this purpose, the need on the high school teacher's part to secure an intimate acquaintance with the beliefs and attitudes of his students is evident.

His most frequent chance to do this thing will probably result from actually listening to what children say, in the classroom and elsewhere. Whenever a child spontaneously offers as his own a statement in propositional form, the indispensable raw material for generating reflection has been provided. The fundamental principle of method which the present theory of the teaching of history implies could be stated as follows:

Any statement by any student which appears to represent a conviction or an idea held (however tentatively) by that student must be eagerly welcomed and taken seriously by the teacher.

The "eager welcoming" of such a statement is not intended to cover such reactions as, "Very good, Johnny—that's a fine contribution. Now who else has an idea?" Rather it means the actual *entertaining* of the idea suggested—the exploration on the spot of its implications, and possibly also of its grounds. When this public consideration of a particular statement seems likely to inhibit rather than to forward an ongoing discussion, the teacher may quite properly content himself with making a note, and promising to explore the idea with the student later; he may also, if he can, throw out a quick example which challenges without demolishing the belief in question and thus draws the student toward more adequate formulation and toward further grounding of his belief. The central point is that whenever a student expresses a judgment, a belief, a conviction, an idea, an opinion, a hypothesis, something *further* ought to happen to it. An expression of some kind which represents the views of the student is the bridge over which the teacher can get inside the student's reflective processes. That bridge is not let down so often that we can afford to miss opportunities; and when the bridge is raised, there is no way of forcing ingress, even with the aid of all the coercive or punitive machinery the school can bring to bear.

Taking a student's belief-statement seriously by no means insures his careful, reflective examination of it; but, at least, it tends to sharpen and refine the statement, and to tighten a little the student's commitment to it. Both of these aspects are important. If a belief is sharply formulated, evidence may far more easily be brought to bear upon it. If commitment to a belief is relatively strong, the raising of evidence that questions it will not result in the student's too easy surrender of his position. Over-eagerness to get at the testing of a student's hypothesis often elicits the reaction, "O.K., then—have it your way. I don't much care, anyway."

The only imaginable reason for reflectively examining a belief is that one has come in some degree to doubt its soundness. And doubt only occasionally arises out of the consciousness of discrepancy between one's own belief and another person's. After all, the proposition "Everyone has a right to his own opinion" is regularly applied to such cases by adults, and is usually taken on by children before pre-adolescence. The effective cause of doubt is rather a discrepancy between one and another of the student's beliefs. However, not all students are emotionally capable of accepting conflict in this form and working it out. The humiliation of a public conviction for inconsistency is often paralyzing. Calling attention to inconsistency in a written paper, on the other hand, often furnishes a powerful stimulus to reflection.

The most effective method of bringing a student's own beliefs to bear upon one another is by the use of hypothetical or actual situations. The student who believes that it is always right to tell the truth may be merely frustrated by the procedure of eliciting an equally unqualified commitment to such an ideal as loyalty, or politeness, or the preservation of human life, and pointing up by examples the inconsistency between his commitments as stated. Often he feels that he has been entrapped, and becomes cagey about expressing his views, thus shutting off from the teacher his most important source of subject-matter. On the other hand, the examples alone, as situations in which the student's belief as stated will not furnish adequate direction, are generally effective in carrying reflection forward. They permit the student to revise a conviction without calling himself mistaken; he is able to feel that the new formulation is "what he really meant in the first place." *After* that revision, the pointing up of the conflict by pulling out from the examples used to challenge his belief the competing values embedded there is much more readily accepted and no less effective in forwarding further reflection.

Getting at the beliefs of students is in last analysis a matter of creating situations in which they may be expressed. The most obvious and fruitful of these are discussion situations and opportunities for writing. However, any situations in which students are free to express valuing attitudes are useful sources, not, indeed, of student beliefs, but of the data against which

hypotheses about student beliefs may be checked. Moreover, if a student can be helped toward consciousness of the values in the light of which he seems to be acting, the elevation of these values to the level of belief is almost a certainty.

Another source for hypotheses as to the probable beliefs of young people is the teacher's knowledge, first of the American culture, and then of the community in which he is working. A third source is his recollection of his own adolescent beliefs, and of those of his friends and associates. A fourth is the observation of groups of students in school situations. This is particularly fruitful if the teacher has a chance to observe his own class group at work with some other teacher, because he can then record on the spot both the hypothesized belief and the behavior from which it was inferred. The richest source of all, however, is the writing done by a student, provided that this writing has been directed toward the free expression of beliefs, attitudes, and values. The posing of emotionally charged situations, described in a paragraph or two, with instructions of the greatest possible simplicity (e.g., "What would you do, and why?" or even "How do you feel about this situation?") ordinarily elicits a limited but appreciable quantity of ready-to-use belief statements, as well as a mass of value-expressions from which beliefs may be inferred or developed through individual conference. The scale-of-belief and problem check list techniques are both useful in this latter connection. Incidentally, the stimulus to participation and "sense of belonging" provided by the use in the classroom, as subject-matter, of materials drawn from student papers is by no means negligible.

It must be kept in mind that the purpose of all the foregoing activities is not to assemble a body of personnel data, although this outcome will surely be a desirable by-product, but rather to generate subject-matter for use in the classroom. The high school teacher of history who is not directing his materials toward the present beliefs of his students, or at least toward certain hypotheses about the nature of these beliefs, is addressing the air or talking to himself; but if he is going to talk to himself anyway, the acme of futility is to run about madly gathering "data" for its own sake. Nor is his obligation in respect to locating student beliefs an unlimited one. When he has all he can actually utilize, this aspect of his job is done; and if half an hour a day, or even fifteen minutes, provides him with as much information on the beliefs of his students as he can actually employ in his work, so much the better.

Moving now toward the teacher's other source of subject-matter, namely, all the history he knows plus whatever else he knows, we shall attempt to see how subject-matter from these two sources may be brought into significant relationships.

It goes without saying that, in order to provide occasions for reflection, the teacher must see that action of some sort is in fact going forward for every student. It may be a very simple type of action, like listening or reading, but it must be *something*. By the same token, the curriculum, however conceived, must provide for something to do. Whether the center of that "something" is the pursuit by each student of some aspect of a unit developed cooperatively by pupil-teacher planning, or the day-by-day examination and discussion of the content of a history text-book, supplemented by other texts, reference books, maps, charts, graphs, films, or recordings makes no particular difference for the purposes of the present study. The question is rather one of how teacher-controlled subject-matter gets into the reflective process, regardless of the particular administrative arrangements under which the history teacher is working.

By way of illustration, let us suppose a world history classroom in which students have encountered, during the reading of an assignment, the statement used in Chapter V to illustrate the extreme of apparently useless information: "Alexander crossed the Hellespont with 35,000 men and began the series of conquests that quickly made him master of Darius' empire."

In the usual course of events, this statement would be "believed" in the limited sense of "not doubted", but nobody would be likely to care much one way or the other about it, except on the off chance that an examination question might call for its regurgitation. Nevertheless, for what it is worth, the students have seen the words and are able after a fashion to visualize some sort of event not inconsistent with them, which is about all the "knowledge of events" anyone ever does get out of a high school text-book.

Suppose, however, that the teacher raises the question, "Could that sentence be a misprint? Surely it doesn't sound reasonable that 35,000 troops could conquer a land containing many millions of people."

That much is enough to get the flow of student hypotheses started. "Maybe there weren't so many people in those days." Investigation will bear this out, but not in sufficient degree to explain Alexander's conquests. "Maybe his army increased as he went along." Investigation supports this also—at least, a student can readily find out that Alexander trained some 30,000 of his conquered subjects in Macedonian military techniques—but again the explanation is quantitatively inadequate. "Maybe the people had no weapons." But Macedonian weapons were not particularly complicated, as the student can easily discover. Vast numbers of people armed with only equipment for hunting, farm implements, clubs, and stones could make a fair showing against a small army. However, a new question could be introduced by the teacher, namely, "Why didn't Darius see to it that every household contained the simple weapons of his day?" Does anyone know why the people of Crete had no arms to combat the German invaders, boys and girls?

Sooner or later, someone will discover that the ordinary inhabitant of an Asiatic empire never took part in wars at all—that he apparently cared not at all who ruled over him. By the time a student has found out why, and has come to compare the passive hopelessness of the natives of Persia with the vigorous self-defence against Persia carried on by the Greek cities a century and a half earlier, and perhaps even to wonder what had enabled Alexander to conquer those same Greek cities, the comparison with the present scene will have become painfully obvious. The state of affairs in India, in Burma, in Egypt, in Malaya, will have become relevant to the idea under discussion, which is no longer Alexander but rather the proposition, "People who believe that they have no stake in their government will not fight to maintain it." The sharp contrast of the Philippines will certainly be drawn, and the meaning of participation explored. The teacher will not, of course, be able to "move forward" in the text-book for many days, but if he sees the creation of a reflective atmosphere, such as has been roughly described, as the primary reason for having the book, he will not be disturbed.[69]

When, however, the class *does* return to the book, and plows ahead over its content, the central idea to which they have leaped, using Alexander as a springboard, is by no means left behind. When they encounter Pyrrhus of Epirus trying to conquer Italy with a small, well-trained force, and find him giving up in disgust because the defeat of one Roman army only meant that another would be sent against him, they may well be impelled to seek in the Roman way of life the qualities that made the common man ready to fight for his country, and to see more clearly than would otherwise have been possible how the slow rise of the common man toward equality and freedom made Rome great, and how the change of direction, resulting, at least in large part, from the accumulation of wealth in a few hands, the extension of slavery, and the growing poverty of the masses, destroyed the common man's commitment-through-participation and finally left Rome at the mercy of authoritarianism and naked force. They will be better able to understand, when they come to it, how the French

Revolution made Carnot's *levée en masse* possible; and the Dutch loss of New Amsterdam will be the old story over again. They may come to understand more realistically the coolness of certain Negro groups to the war effort, and be able to think of sounder remedies than force. They may even come to question whether the threat to national safety of saboteurs and purveyors of sedition exceeds that created by the advocates of poll taxes and Jim Crowism. So far as the writer knows, that question is at the moment an open one.

Or suppose that the students read of how the terramare people brought with them into Italy from the Danube Valley (or Switzerland) a type of settlement built on piles, appropriate to lake-dwellers as a means of insuring safety, but somewhat incongruous on dry land. Was the practice a sheer habit, or had they come to identify safety and security with a method that had once, under utterly different conditions, provided it? Is the latter hypothesis consistent with what we know about history, and with the present day? Shall we turn back toward the Greeks, and the triglyphs on the Parthenon, which represented and resembled the ends of the wooden planks used in the days when temples were made of wood, and which were therefore necessary to a *real* temple, no matter how constructed? Or forward to General Braddock marching his redcoats against the French and their Indian allies in what was at any rate the *correct* formation for an honest-to-goodness army, under all possible conditions? And do we care to laugh—we who, knowing from bitter experience exactly how to operate an economy of scarcity, could do no better when at last we emerged into plenty than to plow under, burn, slaughter, destroy until scarcity had been regained and our cherished habits could work again? Can the terramare people top that one? And who recalls our smug certainty that war in Europe was impossible because we had all the money and would virtuously refuse to lend them any? And so we are off after illustrations of the cultural lag; we are out to learn whether men have consistently loved their habits better than their dreams, their aspirations, their neighbors' welfare, and even the protection of their own lives. We shall look also for occasions when necessary transitions have been made; perhaps it is only in some areas that we persist in keeping on with obviously inept procedures. Has it *always* required a revolution to shake off the dead hand of tradition? Can we learn to loose its grip before the rigor mortis of reaction stiffens and tightens it?

The multiplication of examples is pointless. Enough has been said to indicate what is meant by the use of historical materials in reflection. The heart of the method is to point up an apparent conflict (e.g., the size of Alexander's army and the apparent magnitude of the forces against him, seen in the light of the student's prior experience with unequal numbers in combat) in such a way as to elicit explanatory hypotheses. Once that has been done, the testing of the hypotheses will call into action all relevant facts, historical or drawn from current situations, that anyone in the group knows or can dig up. It matters not at all whether we start with a fact encountered in an ordinary, prosaic history assignment, a unit topic, or a present-day problem, so long as we move at once toward the evocation of directing hypotheses which will order and arrange both the materials out of which we generated our initial question mark and an indefinitely large body of other materials employed to test our hypotheses.

The subject-matter which the teacher controls enables him to do three important things, namely:

(1) He is able to direct students who seek to ground hypotheses toward materials that will carry their thinking forward.

(2) He is able, at appropriate points, to "toss in" the precise bits of information necessary to give impetus to a student's examination of a hypothesis. He can challenge an idea that seems headed toward too ready acceptance, or support one worthy of consideration that is about to be dismissed as patently false.

(3) The fact that he can often adduce relevant information enables him without constraint to admit the lack of it. In this way he can strike a blow against the acceptance of authority as omniscient, and focus the reliance of the group, not upon the teacher's sure knowledge, but upon the method which he and they are both applying.

It is vitally important, however, that the teacher should not restrict his contributions to materials drawn from books. The teacher of American history who has shown to his class the film "The Story That Couldn't Be Printed", which presents the trial of Peter Zenger, can get reflection stirring in useful directions by pointing out that Zenger both owned and edited his paper. In a day when this situation was common, the freedom of a professional newspaperman to speak his mind was adequately protected if the courts would uphold the first amendment and similar provisions (wherever they existed) in state constitutions. Is an editor free to speak his mind today? From there we could head either toward the reliance on safeguards built to meet conditions that have disappeared, or toward the specific question of what social arrangements might now provide freedom of the press in the sense in which the first amendment once provided it, or toward an examination of the Bill of Rights to see what other parts of it have suffered loss of meaning through changing social conditions, or toward an examination of newspapers and periodicals to determine the extent to which they seek to provide the facts people need in order to participate effectively in the solution of today's problems, and the extent to which they seem to seek specific behaviors on the part of their readers, or toward a consideration of the kinds of values which impel men to risk the displeasure of constituted authorities, or, doubtless, in many other directions. The determination of direction is limited by the hypotheses or beliefs which a discussion of the film elicits from students; within those limits, the teacher must select the direction that seems most promising, in terms of his best guess as to what each line of attack may lead into.

If his class had seen the film "Land of Liberty", the teacher could pull out Otis' stirring contention that fair taxation is more important than national unity, and throw against it that part of the film in which Jackson is shown as insisting that national unity is more important than fair taxation. Both statements appear to be offered as absolute principles, and both appear to be approved in the American tradition. The reconciliation of this conflict by an examination of the circumstances surrounding both speeches, and the attempt to find a more adequate controlling principle, might easily develop into highly profitable experiences.

If the film were "Sons of Liberty", the teacher could, if he had the courage, pull out the episode of the poor widow who gave her last four hundred dollars to the Revolutionary cause in the conviction that God would look after her, and raise the question whether a more genuine respect for God's power would not have been shown had she kept her four hundred dollars and asked God to look after General Washington.

The films discussed above are literally loaded with similar potential conflicts; the writer has never seen a film dealing with history, prepared or adapted for school use, which did not contain at least four sharp and readily discernible conflicts of ideals, beliefs, or values.

Any use that can be made of commercial films is particularly desirable, as suggesting to students that relevant material from all sources is welcome. What they hear on the radio, what they read in newspapers or magazines, what happened to them at the swimming pool or the circus or the wrestling match, must become respectable as potential subject-matter, and, in a society that makes children conservative long before it permits them to drive cars, the teacher will have to take the lead in bringing that respectability into being. Students cannot integrate their experiences through reflection if a large part of those experiences are somehow deemed unworthy in the situation out of which reflection grows. Indeed, other things being equal, it will be better if the teacher can actually drawn relevant or suggestive illustrations from Charlie McCarthy than from Raymond Gram Swing, from Zane Gray than from Joseph Conrad, from the comic strips which the student does read than from the editorials which the student does not read.

The writer has said that he sees no clear reason for concern over whether the center of the day-to-day activity into which reflection must cut is a course of study or a text-book on the one hand, or a consideration of present-day problems on the other. This statement, however, means only that the writer is not concerned with where we *begin*. The teacher must bring historical materials into relation with the beliefs of students, and therefore with present-day problems; but he must not forget what is ancillary to what. The only defensible reason for studying history is still what it has always been: to shed light on the quandaries of our life today.

If the human life-span were longer, what has been said in this chapter would perhaps be adequate to indicate the implications for curriculum and method of the theory outlined in Chapter V. As stated so far, the proposal appears to be, "Help students to ground their beliefs in experience through reflective thinking. Use for this purpose any subject-matter that happens to be accessible, out of the experience of the students or the teacher, out of the materials of the course, or from any other source as it may be encountered. The only test for subject-matter will be the test of relevance to a belief under examination."

The foregoing statement suggests that we are trying to provide for the student an opportunity to build his own frame of reference; and so, in a sense, we are. At any rate, we are trying to give the student control of the method by which a frame of reference is constructed. It looks plausible to suggest that our job is solely to equip him with the method, and then to let him find his own way. In the language of one of the more recent clichés, we should teach him "how and not what to think."

The apparent neutrality of this formulation is quite spurious. When we focus upon the reflective method in the history class, we affirm clearly that frames of reference are properly built and modified through reflection. On what basis do we affirm this? It is denied in practice all over the world. Even in America, many agencies are eager to cause children to accept particular beliefs, without reflection; some even go so far as to want facts *kept out* of a student's experience if their evidential tendency is toward some conclusion which is regarded as undesirable. The view that reflection should enter into the construction of one's own frame of reference, and that no area ought to be withheld from reflective scrutiny, is *itself* a part of democracy's positive and distinctive frame of reference. Bringing the student toward an exclusive reliance upon reflection as the test of truth is teaching him "what to think" with a vengeance; and the only reason why we do not vigorously indoctrinate that point of view is because the desired end cannot be obtained in that way. Teaching students to think, as a goal, implies that something will be done about the fact that the process of walling off areas of experience from the impact of thought is going on continuously all around the student. Just as reflection is democracy's method for reaching judgments, so walling off of preferred values is the method of authoritarianism for protecting specific beliefs from examination. Unless, through reflection, the student can be brought to see the issue thus posed and to take a stand on it, he cannot build for himself a frame of reference that is other than authoritarian.

This point is so basic that the writer, at risk of laboring the obvious, feels impelled to develop it again from another angle. It is true that the student who has had experience in the use of reflective thinking will develop a certain habitual reliance upon the method. But it is clear that reflection, which is a technique for applying the tests of experience to purported knowledge, is valid only where the tests of experience are valid. Standards and values which arise out of experience may be tested by experience. Standards and values arising anywhere else— "laws of nature" built into the structure of the universe, or created by the fiat of some Being outside space and time—are obviously beyond the reach of experience, and therefore not subject to reflective examination. The only possible guarantee of continued and exclusive reliance upon reflective or scientific method as the way of finding truth and of making judgments of practice is therefore a positive frame of reference which includes the conviction that standards and values arise out of human experience, and that they do not arise in any other way, no matter what men may claim for them. Once that principle is established, the validity of any standard is determined and maintained through the participation of people in its continuous, reflective examination in the light of its consequences for the common concerns of the group. Conflict of standards thus leads to a widening of the groups involved, at a new level of realization. The alternatives to this method of resolving conflict are violence or the isolation of groups from one another, totally or with respect to selected areas of experience.

It is entirely possible that, given time, any individual who could think reflectively, and whose experience included some portion of democratic living, would arrive independently at the democratic point of view. But men do not live for a thousand years.

The reflective examination of any proposition tends to develop skill in the use of the method. The reflective examination of a belief to which one is committed tends to develop a reliance on reflection as a method of securing truth. But if we are headed in the direction of enabling the student at some time to choose his way of life, to make his decision as between democracy and one or another of the available competing authoritarianisms, we need to act positively in terms of that purpose.

For this reason, it is necessary to include with what has been said three additional principles:

1. So far as possible, any belief under examination should be placed in clear opposition to other beliefs in the culture which are or appear to be inconsistent with it.
2. So far as possible, students should be brought to see conflicts among their beliefs as exemplifying familiar controversial issues.
3. So far as possible, subject-matter drawn from those areas which are most sharply controversial within our culture should be deliberately preferred over equality evidential but relatively less highly charged subject-matter.

The repeated phrase, "so far as possible" is meant to call attention to the fact that every procedure suggested above is dangerous, in that it may incur the violent opposition of powerful groups. We have, however, reached the point where refusal to make the distinction between democracy and authoritarianism clear is even more dangerous. Even at some risk, we must seize the limited chance we still have to build for a world fit for free men to live in.

An illustration of what is meant by the three principles stated above may be in place here. Let us suppose that a class is reading what the textbook has to say about the election of 1800. There will surely be something on the bitterness of the campaign, and on the horrible consequences predicted for the country if Jefferson, "a radical and an atheist," were elected.

A teacher may cut in here, in discussion, to raise the question, "Do you suppose these people—Dwight, for example—believed what they said? Or did they just make those things up for the election?" Groups will divide sharply on this question, some insisting that the sheer extravagance of the Federalist charges (the teacher may have to augment these, since texts often go easy at this point) reveals them as propaganda, while others insist that men like Adams

and Hamilton would not deliberately be false to what they thought.

Now suppose that the teacher injects a new question: "If men really believe that the election of a given candidate will ruin the country, how far are they justified in going, out of sheer patriotism, to prevent his election?"

Some ideas will emerge here toward which the example of Hamilton's famous letter to Jay may be addressed. "Suppose, for the sake of argument, that Hamilton was perfectly sincere in believing that Jefferson's election would be disastrous. Now consider this: among the papers of John Jay (time out for "Who remembers Jay? What did he do?" etc.) was a letter from Hamilton, written just before this election of 1800. It asks Jay, as Governor of New York, to juggle the election laws (time out for, "Have you ever heard of that before? Tell about it. What's a 'gerrymander'? What happened recently to Congressman Eliot, of Massachusetts? etc.) in such a way as to insure a Federalist victory no matter what the people wanted (time out for "How could he do that?" discussion of electoral college, etc.). Now, then, what do you think of Hamilton's proposal? If he was trying to save his country from a horrible fate, wasn't he justified (time out for fairly heated forensics, largely ungrounded)?"

After a while, the teacher interjects, "Jay left a note on the envelope of that letter. It said, 'A proposal for party purposes which it would ill become me to consider.' How do you react to that?"

The point must be made clear that Jay agreed with Hamilton as to the character and extent of the disaster Jefferson's election would cause. It should also be made clear that the Federalists, being in power rather generally, could have followed Hamilton's suggestion with some success, and driven Jefferson's followers to submission or revolution as their only alternatives. Secondary school students probably cannot formulate the difference between Jay's outlook and Hamilton's, but they sense it readily and show some insight into its quality. They rarely condemn Hamilton out of hand, though; they seem to understand how loyalty to a set of fixed standards may compel that kind of behavior.

Other aspects of the same situation may be used in the same direction. Dwight was trying to save the country from the horrors of an atheist president. Has an atheist a right to run for president? Does the freedom of religion we are fighting for include the freedom to have no religion? Did Americans of the eighteenth century feel more friendly toward atheism than people do today? Why wouldn't Philadelphia permit a statue to Tom Paine? What kind of president did Jefferson turn out to be? What were the religious views of Benjamin Franklin? Of George Washington? (This last is perhaps *too* risky—if the youngsters find out, they'll probably bubble over in the wrong places. However, only the very diligent are likely to find out anything on this point until many years later.)

Some reference in this connection to the practice in many states of barring certain political parties from the ballot may also be related to the Hamilton-Jay business. The economic make-up of the Federalist party also has utility here, and a quick look back over Adams' administration, emphasizing the alien and sedition laws and Adams' immigration policy, will yield quantities of evidential material.

One may treat the election of 1800 in scholarly and thorough fashion without upsetting anyone and without doing more than skirt the edges of controversy. One may even promote a fair amount of thinking that way. But the intent to develop, through thinking, a frame of reference that *relies on* thinking, will make certain ideas and events seem almost to pop out of the pages of the text or out of our own remembered reading.

Our method is the promotion of reflective thinking; moreover, we do not hope that students will have a solid grip on the democratic ideal as the result of their high school study of history. But the intent to bring them toward the conscious choice between authoritarianism and democracy will condition our choice of materials and our methods every step of the way.

VII
THE SUBJECT-MATTER PREPARATION
OF TEACHERS OF HISTORY

We have seen that the role of teacher-controlled subject-matter in the secondary school history class is to carry reflective thinking forward; that it does this by playing, within the experience of the high school student, the role of needed evidence; that "learning history" means "creating, out of the materials of history, some of the tests and grounds for the beliefs in the light of which we operate."

We know, then, what we expect teachers of history to do with subject-matter. The present question is, "What kind of subject-matter preparation seems likely to help them to do it?

The most obvious implication of the theory elaborated in this study is that *subject-matter which teachers expect to use in promoting reflection should have been learned through reflection.* If the prospective teacher of history has not used historical materials to test the validity of his own beliefs, attitudes, and values, and as a source of hypotheses about the relation of man to his institutions and social arrangements, he simply does not know the materials *that way*; nor does he know how to go on generating subject-matter out of his reading or his daily living.

A second principle must be added hastily, however, which will condition the application of the first: *the prospective teacher's subject-matter preparation should be carried on in the light of his intent subsequently to use subject-matter for the promotion of reflective thinking on the part both of students and of the prospective teacher himself.*

At the college level, a fairly common interpretation of the expression "learning a body of knowledge" is "accepting, either on faith or as fairly secure hypotheses, the assertions contained in the materials, and going on to find and test meaning *for* them." Some reflective activity of this kind certainly does go on and has gone on throughout the history of education.

There is, moreover, a very real sense in which this kind of activity is indispensable to human progress, although it certainly belongs at the college level and perhaps even at the graduate level. One of the most effective defenses for a traditional conception of subject-matter runs something like this:

"We cannot expect college students to go through the processes by which our present knowledge in science, history, or mathematics came into being. Nor is any such impossible repetition of the work of our forbears necessary. If it were, progress would be at a standstill; for no man could repeat in a lifetime the experiences through which our knowledge in a single field was acquired. Indeed, it would be a life work to test all the assumptions upon which we operate in a single *corner* of a field of knowledge, such as organic chemistry or Roman history.

"Obviously, it would be desirable if everybody could know everything for himself; but human limitations and the shortness of the life-span suggest that it is a good deal more sensible to take as assured the knowledge which is handed to us in condensed and organized form by competent authorities, and then to go forward to find new meanings for our tradition. We thus add *new* knowledge to the knowledge we are 'given', and the increment from generation to generation is one possible measure of progress."

We may grant at once that life has been greatly enriched by the accumulated learnings of the past. Most of us drive motor-cars no one generation could have built, wear textiles into whose creation have gone decades of chemical research, avail ourselves of drugs and medicines whose development spans many lifetimes. The products we enjoy because of our "building upon the accumulated knowledge of the past" have amply justified a continuation of the process.

However, as James Harvey Robinson points out,[70] this "accumulated knowledge" is often stored in libraries where only experts know how to find it and what to do with it. The scientists who are going to carry modern physics forward from its present level are certainly going to be a small group of remarkable individuals whose rare native endowments have been developed through a long and highly specialized preparation. No undergraduate subject-matter can do much more for these embryonic savants, with regard to their subsequent contributions to human knowledge, than to catch their interest and perhaps direct it toward further experiences in the same area.

The conclusion that the job of adding to our "accumulated knowledge" ought to be carried on is by no means a justification for acting as if all college students were going to work at *that* job rather than at any of the countless other tasks which likewise have to be done. We are confronted today by the spectacle of a highly literate nation, famous for its contributions to "knowledge", engaged in the business, first, of limiting both the growth and the authority of that "knowledge", and second, of using its fruits to enslave the minds of a nation and to spread terror and destruction over a whole continent. In our own country, we have once faced—and may face again—the necessity of destroying the foods we have learned, through arduous effort over many generations, to grow in abundance; of plowing under the cotton whose production and utilization embody countless hours of laborious research. The simple "increase of human knowledge", in the sense in which that term has been used above, is by no means the sole or even as of today an important problem of general education. Even if the contribution of undergraduate work to this increase were more than infinitesimal, we would not justify operating in terms of it as a central purpose.

It must be recognized, however, that the aims of developing historical scholars and of furthering the purposes of those students who simply "like history" are perfectly legitimate ones. Moreover, the kind of control which a teacher needs of his subject-matter, namely, the ability to recall and to apply in other contexts the detailed facts which have served him as evidence in building his own beliefs and ideas into a point of view, is no particular desideratum for the ordinary student of history in a college or university. When, as is generally the case, the prospective teacher's subject-matter courses are taken as something quite discrete from his work in the field of education, a professional control of materials is ordinarily not even sought, and can be obtained only in occasionally and almost accidental cases.

There is certainly nothing to be gained by instituting special courses for teachers whose content is confined to materials which are appropriate for high school students. That sort of activity is of course inescapably necessary, on the job; and when it is carried on to the exclusion of a normal, adult contact with the world's knowledge, it sometimes makes teachers in service look to other adults like cases of arrested development.

E. S. Evenden is probably quite right in suggesting that, ideally:

[A professionalized subject-matter course] for teachers is first of all subject-matter—accurate, scholarly, and of a degree of difficulty to challenge students at the level the course is offered, comparable in most of its content to the context of similar courses offered to students other than prospective teachers in colleges and universities.

In the second place, it is taught by an instructor who has a scholarly command of his field and in addition to scholarship has secured, either by experience or extended observation of public-school teaching, a sensitiveness to the problems of teaching his subject to children of different ages and varied interests. He should also know enough about educational psychology, tests and measurements in his subject, and other similar professional material to be able to apply that information in his questions, in his illustrative comments, in his special assignments, in his demonstration lessons, in his examinations—in other words, in his teaching.

In the third place, it is subject-matter selected, whenever opportunities for selection exist, because the unit chosen will have more direct or indirect effect upon the work of the prospective teacher taking the course than other units which might be selected. This selection cannot be made except by instructors whose knowledge of the subject is sufficiently thorough to supply material from which to choose and who at the same time know the work of the public schools well enough to supply the criteria for those choices.

In the fourth place, it is subject-matter selected for teachers who should be leaders in their communities, who should realize the important rôle the schools will be called upon to play in molding citizens for a complex and changing civilization, who should be made conscious of the part the subject-matter of that course can take in that molding, and who should develop personal interests which will contribute to their intellectual, social, and recreational life as individuals. The subject-matter of the course should contribute, whenever possible, to some of all those needs.[71]

The sort of person Evenden wants for instructor, however, will surely be hard to find. In any case, only a few institutions have attempted differentiated courses for teachers; as a rule they follow the policy of "providing general courses in subject-matter, with the responsibility for furnishing the teacher's professional equipment delegated to the professors of education...."[72]

For two reasons, then—because of existing institutional patterns and because of the extreme difficulty of finding men who could keep dif-ferentiated history courses for teachers from degenerating into either methods courses or straight subject-matter—this study does not propose the so-called "professionalized subject-matter" course. In any case, no history course, however taught, would be likely to bring the prospective history teacher's other chief source of potential subject-matter—the beliefs of his prospective students—into the picture.

It is obvious that no prospective teacher can hope to learn in advance the precise beliefs which his prospective students will hold. He is justified, however, in assuming that the groups he will some day teach will not be utterly different from other youngsters maturing within much the same culture.

The initial proposal of this study for the subject-matter preparation of history teachers, therefore, is that all students, as soon as possible after they have decided to prepare for the teaching of history, be brought into contact with the people who presumably will have to do with them, some day, in student teaching and in methods courses. So far as it can be done in one or two interviews and a group meeting, the importance of clear hypotheses about students' beliefs should be indicated, and a series of assignments lined up somewhat as follows:

(1) A listing of "Things I Think Young People Believe Today"
(2) "Some of the Things I Used to Believe in High School"
(3) "Some of the Things My Friends in High School Used to Believe"
(4) A series of observations carried on with the intent to infer student beliefs from what they say and do in the classroom.
(5) A check-up, in which the student will have the responsibility for establishing contact with young people and finding chances to talk with them about his ideas of what youngsters believe. The intent is for the student to see how well he has guessed or inferred.

Due dates will be set in such a way that occasional conferences during this series of activities will be possible. For some students, an acquaintance even in this preliminary stage with some of the literature of adolescent psychology and sociology may be appropriate.

During the following quarter or semester, the entire group will be required to register for a particular history course, chosen from among the courses already required. Enrollment in this course for education students will not be permitted without the recommendation of the faculty member or members in charge of the area dealing with the teaching of history.

Concurrently with this selected history course, over whose procedures and content the college or department of education will attempt to exercise no control and very little influence, the group will be required to register for a course in methods in the teaching of history. This course will confine itself to a steady consideration of the question, "What can we do, specifically, with the content of our required history course?"

At first the course should appear to focus simply upon the finding of materials which have an evidential bearing upon a belief which some member of the class considers likely to be held by some of his prospective students. This approach is almost certain to dissolve into a consideration of the relevance of history materials to beliefs actually held by members of the group—and this fact is all to the good. The ostensible focus should be on identifying evidential relationships until most of the class can do it with some facility; actually, the prospective teacher will simply have an additional opportunity for making reflective use of the course materials on his own account. This is presumably, and often actually, what the history instructor wants him to do; the motivating drive of professional preparation is thus placed squarely behind the efforts of the subject-matter area, rather than reserved exclusively for the so-called professional courses. Until students have learned to make conscious use of subject-matter materials in constructing their own points of view, they are not ready to begin learning to help others do so.

That point having been reached by a considerable proportion of the class, the emphasis will be modified by a second set of questions, namely, "How can I get what I have learned, and can see as evidentially related to a belief, into a form that is intelligible to high school students? Is this material likely to be in their text-books? If so, is there enough characteristic detail to permit them, with some help, to catch the evidential relationship I have caught? Can they find the material somewhere else in language they can read? Can I put it into that kind of language?

At the conclusion of this course, which should come before the end of the sophomore year, each student who has failed to show at least some capacity for perceiving the relationship of evidence to propositions will be told quite frankly that his ability to achieve certification as a history teacher is highly doubtful, and that he could well consider turning his energies in some other direction. A written memorandum of this conference should be signed by both student and instructor and dropped in the student's file. For those who wish to go on with the attempt, a particular advanced course in history will be agreed upon by the group concerned, and all members of the group will register for this course during a designated quarter or semester of the junior year. Through individual conferences or in a weekly group meeting, depending upon numbers involved, the instructor in the teaching of history will continue his previously unsuccessful efforts to develop the capacity for reflective use of materials.

Those who still "don't get it" should at this point be told that, while they are entitled to keep on trying, they will not be admitted to additional work in the teaching of history until they can demonstrate the competence necessary for going ahead.

All students who have successfully completed their basic course will be required to register for a course dealing with the reflective use in history teaching of materials drawn from sources other than history texts. Films and recordings will probably be utilized first, and technical instruction in the use of equipment can probably fit in here if it is not provided for elsewhere in the student's required program. Course work in other areas than history, commercial films, radio programs, plays, lectures, newspapers, and magazines will be utilized by students as sources of teacher-controlled subject-matter; newspapers, magazines, and children's literature will be examined as sources of evidential material directly accessible (in the sense that the teacher can refer to it and even provide it) to high school students.

With regard to patterning the subject-matter courses history teachers ought to take, not much is known by anyone. Obviously, course work in history should bulk fairly large, representing perhaps the rough equivalent of a year's work as a minimum, with no top limit at all. A clear implication of the theory outlined in this study is an increased emphasis on advanced courses loaded with characteristic detail, as against beginning courses which are more often the "broad survey" kind of thing that is more appropriate to indicating the relationship of a wide range of already-learned materials to each other than to securing the learning, through reflection, of useful parts of its own content.

A second clear implication is that sociology and anthropology should be required in a quantity approaching (in combination) the history requirement itself. There is a sense in which the theory advanced in this study involves the conversion of history by the student into a kind of sociology. The emphasis proposed upon such matters as race, religion, moral and ethical standards, nationalism, and economic life clearly calls for rich resources built up more readily from the materials of sociology and anthropology than from any subject-matter source except history itself.

Economics is certainly a significant related area, but again the advanced courses have preference over the usual elementary courses, even for the beginner. A course dealing with the economic ideas, notions, and superstitions of our culture, or a course which developed classical economic theory and steadily tested it against experience in the light of its adequacy to explain and to predict would be of tremendous value.

Some work in political science is customary and probably desirable. A number of institutions provide courses in the "engineering of consent", or the formation of public opinion, and these are so useful for our purpose that the necessary prerequisites, if not too time-consuming, are probably worth while. So are courses which deal frankly with political theory, contrasting it with practice wherever possible. Beginning courses in political science, not too many years ago, sometimes presented a single political theory as if it were a description of something in experience; if, as is possible so far as the writer knows, such courses have wholly disappeared, the history teacher can make good use of the political science area. Where a course dealing in any significant degree with history of law can be found, it should be required for history teachers.

Geography as a natural science has no special status so far as the proposals of this study are concerned. Geography treated as the influence of physical environment on human behavior should of course be recommended. American and English literature, and especially poetry, because of the ease with which it can be injected into a classroom situation, are likely to be fertile sources of material. For the rest, anything a history teacher can learn about any subject may be of use.

The proposals of this study will of course be much facilitated if a formal course in the nature of the reflective process is available to undergraduates prior to their student-teaching experiences. If this recommendation seems to conflict with the earlier proposal that students should come at the nature of reflection in the process of their subject-matter preparation, it is because of the same old language trick discussed in Chapter IV. A formal course in reflective thinking *as a beginning point* would be absurd; but the need *at some point* to pull the process out and look at it is an implication of the intent to develop teachers who can promote reflection not only through habitual ways of handling materials, but *on purpose.*

Student teaching would change somewhat in emphasis under the theory proposed, because whenever the curriculum is regarded as hypothesis some provision for estimating its adequacy is essential. Early in the course of his student teaching experience—but not *prior* to it in any systematic sense—the prospective teacher must come to grips with the question, "How do I tell whether I am getting anywhere?" If the question does not arise in this form, the necessity in most schools for giving tests of some sort and the tremendous difficulties of constructing tests that have any clear relation to what he is trying to do are certain to bring it up.

The writer believes that basic courses in education, which generally give a lick and a promise (occasionally more) to tests and measurements, could well refrain from doing even that. The ground for this view is that as soon as a student has come to think of testing as a discrete process, susceptible of meaningful treatment outside the matrix of purposes and plans within which the imperious need for testing arises, he has become to some extent callous to that need. He knows "how to make a test," and that fact may give him a kind of security, but it is the security of familiarity rather than of understanding. The writer's recommendation would be that the course in tests and measurements, if one is offered, should be concurrent with student teaching, and that if such a course is not offered, the time devoted to student teaching should be augmented to warrant two or three additional semester hours of credit, in order to make room for individualized work in evaluation, addressed sharply to the situation in which the student is working.

It may be observed that no reference has been made in these pages to courses in special methods in teaching history. The omission is deliberate. The writer believes that a student who is clear as to purpose, not in the sense of being able to state his personal philosophy, but in the sense of having control of a theory, and who has observed many teachers at work, will manufacture method as he goes along. He believes even that in last analysis clarity of purpose, fertility of hypotheses as to method, and insight into the function of evaluation are the minimum essentials of method that is progressive in the sense of being continually adapted to purpose and situation.

In general, then, the proposals for the subject-matter preparation of history teachers which are offered in this chapter are predicated upon certain assumptions about the kind of professional preparation available. Apart from these assumptions, the suggestions made here have no practical significance.

It must be remembered also that to work in the light of any theory is a choice. An institution can properly require any individual to demonstrate that he understands a theory and is capable of applying it. It can require no more than that. A student is entitled, as a free citizen, to take any attitude he may care to take toward such a theory as the one sponsored in this study, so long as he can demonstrate control over it, and thus create the presumption that his choice really is a choice.

Because the teacher who does choose to work in the light of the theory here presented will necessarily be headed at all times toward controversial and therefore dangerous areas, he has a right to the facts before making his choice. The suggestions offered in this chapter presuppose the existence of a vigorous and sympathetic department or area in educational philosophy which will be concerned with pushing students toward a consideration of fundamental choices in the light of their probable consequences. Since colleges of education are not prepared to underwrite the living expenses of their graduates during periods of unemployment resulting from insufficient caution in doing what they have been taught to do, the obligation to make the prospective teacher aware of what he is doing is clear and urgent. It is also an institutional responsibility; acquainting the student with what he may expect must be someone's job, and the responsibility must be clear and definite, even in institutions where Howard Beale's "Are American Teachers Free?" is on a dozen required-reading lists. So far as it can be done, any educational institution in a democracy has the responsibility of freeing individuals from the danger of being entrapped by their own nurture and led into risks they would not wilfully have run. No one should ever "find himself" out on a limb; free men are entitled to the privilege of clambering out on purpose, for the sake of values which make the possible dangers, cooly appraised, seem worth incurring.

NOTES

[1] Committee on the Function of Science in General Education of the Commission on Secondary School Curriculum, *Science in General Education*, p. 24.

[2] *Ibid.*, pp. 146–152

[3] Twenty-six states now have legislation requiring the teaching of American history. See Nevins, Alan: "American History for Americans", *New York Times Magazine*, May 3, 1942, p. 6.

[4] The writer knows of a few exceptions, and there must be still others of which he has not heard.

[5] "Time" here is used to refer to "credit hours". In terms of actual hours of study, there is good reason to suppose that the proportion may be considerably higher.

[6] Trotter, William: *Instincts of the Herd in Peace and War*, p. 44

[7] Fraser, Sir John, *The Golden Bough*, p. 22.

[8] Horn, Ernest: *Methods of Instruction in the Social Studies*; p. 4.

[9] Beard, Charles A.: *The Nature of the Social Studies*, pp. 193–230.

[10] Wesley, E. B.: *Teaching the Social Studies*, pp. 84–89. Italics not in original.

[11] Bining, A. C., Mohr, W. H., and McFeely, R. H.: *Organizing the Social Studies in Secondary Schools*, p. 64.

[12] Seignobos, Charles: *The Secondary Teaching of History in France*, Revue Universitaire, 1896, Vol. 1, Tr. by G. G. Berry in *Introduction to the Study of History*, p. 331.

[13] Johnson, Henry: *An Introduction to the History of the Social Sciences in Schools*, p. 97.

[14] Beard, Charles A.: "That Noble Dream", *American Historical Review*, xli, October, 1935, p. 87.

[15] Smith, Theodore Clarke: "Writing of American History in America, from 1884 to 1934", *American Historical Review*, xl, April, 1935, p. 440.

[16] For a striking exception, see Beard, Robinson and Smith, *Our Own Age*, pp. 5–14.

[17] Langlois, Charles V., and Seignobos, Charles: *Introduction to the Study of History*, p. 115.

[18] For this and many other examples both of the ingenuity and of the relative aimlessness of a certain kind of scholarship, see Dennis, George: *Cities and Cemeteries of Etruria*.

[19] Fay, Sidney: *The Origins of the World War*, Vol. II., *After Sarajevo: Immediate Causes of the War*, pp. 167–182.

[20] Beard, Charles A.: *op. cit.*, p. 75.

[21] Langlois, *op. cit.*, p. 18.

[22] except, of course, as small groupings of facts serve to test one another.

[23] Langlois and Seignobos; *op. cit.*, p. 262.

[24] *Ibid.*, p. 263.

[25] *Ibid.*, p. 264.

[26] Seignobos says, "This, indeed, is what a historian is compelled to do,....but he does not say so to avoid scandal." *Ibid.*, p. 231.

[27] Carlyle and Michelet are egregious illustrations of this tendency; no historian can wholly escape it.

[28] Quoted by Henry Johnson, *An Introduction to the History of the Social Sciences in Schools*, p. 21.

[29] Ellis, Edward Sylvester: *Young People's History of Our Country*, p. vi.

[30] Johnson, Henry: *op. cit.*, p. 126.

[31] Langlois and Seignobos, *op. cit.*, p. 331.

[32] *Ibid.*, p. 331.

[33] Nevins, Allen: "American History for Americans", *New York Times Magazine*, May 3, 1942.

[34] Craven, Avery: *Democracy in American Life*, p. 143.

[35] Duvall, T. G.: *Great Thinkers*, p. 47.

[36] Curti, Margaret W.: *Child Psychology*, p. 337.

[37] Cook, Edgar Marion: *An Analysis of the Methods Used in Solving a Rational Learning Problem*, George Peabody College for Teachers, Nashville, Tenn., p. 8.

[38] Franz, Shepherd Ivory; Layman, John D.; Kilduff, Sybil; Morgan, Roy C.; Davis, Evalene F.; Eaton, Amerette G.; McCulloch, T. L.: *The Possibility of Space Perception by Tactile Means*, University of California Press, Berkeley, California, p. 91, 1933.

[39] Balken, Eva Ruth: *Affective, Volitional and Galvanic Factors in Learning*. Part of Ph.D. Thesis, Department of Psychology, 1930, The University of Chicago Libraries, Chicago, Illinois, Reprinted from the Journal of Experimental Psychology, Vol. xvi, No. 1, Feb. 1933, p. 115.

[40] The writer confesses at once that he has no notion what the word "desirable" in this context could possibly mean; he is simply trying to use language which will evoke a *sense* of the position he is attacking, a position in which he is unable to find intelligible meaning so far as matters of valuing, or "desirability", are concerned.

[41] Some may say that the foregoing paragraphs are an attack on a "straw man", and that no important number of teachers are operating on the basis of attempting to inculcate specific habits. Proof on the point is not available. The writer has been observing schools and talking with teachers for fifteen years, and he believes that some of

them work on the basis described above.

[42]To anyone who cares to argue that democracy *can* do these things, I can only reply that in that case I find no differences between a democratic society and a totalitarian state; differences in the *specific content* of the value hierarchy will not support any such distinction, since they are common enough as *between* any two dictatorships.

[43]Cf. Russell, Bertrand: *An Inquiry into Meaning and Truth*, Chapter iii.

[44]Trotter, William: *Instincts of the Herd in Peace and War*, p. 45.

[45]Robinson, James Harvey: *The Mind in the Making, The Relation of Intelligence to Social Reform*, pp. 58–59.

[46]*Ibid.*, p. 60.

[47]By "on demand" is here meant "whenever the belief is actually called into question either by the facts of a given situation or by a conflict with another belief which suggests a different course of action", rather than "whenever anyone asks us to examine our beliefs."

[48]It is, of course, possible for an authoritarian state to wrap the new beliefs in a special set of emotional appeals so intense that they will supplant beliefs of longer standing; but this process can scarcely be used on a large scale more than once in a generation. In any case, this possibility is at best a last desperate resort, so far as democracy is concerned.

[49]Dewey, John: *How We Think*, p. 6.

[50]Whether much of it can be converted from "potential information" into knowledge is a question on which men may easily differ *a priori*. The attempt to accomplish this conversion, undertaken on a large scale, would presumably answer the question, and at the same time determine whether there is a place for history in the school curriculum.

[51]This illustration is developed in Chapter VI, p. 179.

[52]We say also, of course, that a child who has "learned" to ride a bicycle "knows how to" ride one. But in this sense, "know" would be translated into Latin not as "scire" or even "cognoscere" but rather as "posse" or at the most "discere". The idea that whoever "can" must perforce "know how to" is familiar; but we admit readily enough that the coach who "knows how to" play football frequently can't.

[53]Kilpatrick, W. H.: *Re-making the Curriculum*; p. 50.

[54]As will appear, these criteria are of a character that destroys the seeming "objectivity" of the present definition of "attitude". Cf. p. 34.

[55]This assumption has been defended in Chapter IV.

[56]The difference here is very close to Dewey's distinction between sheer "opinion" and "judgment", as expressed in "Logic; the Theory of Inquiry", p. 122.

[57]The relation of behavior to an imputed attitude actually comes fairly close to the relation of a check to a bank-account. Neither behavior nor check refers to an "entity" in the sense in which a parking-check has an "entity" behind it; both are merely ways of ordering and arranging our expectations about the behavior of other people.

[58]Witness the plaint of a thousand popular songs, "I want someone to care for."

[59]That is to say, if valuing is extended to include repulsion as well as attraction, then a value is simply that toward which an attitude is taken.

[60]Quoted by Rattner, Joseph, *John Dewey's Philosophy*, facing page.

[61]Dewey, John: *How We Think*, p. 72.

[62]Kilpatrick, W. H.: *Remaking the Curriculum*, p. 68.

[63]*Ibid.*, p. 48–50.

[64]*Ibid.*, p. 49.

[65]*Ibid.*, p. 49.

[66]Columbia Associates in Philosophy: *An Introduction to Reflective Thinking*, p. 334.

[67]Dewey, John, *How We Think*, p. 8.

[68]This statement, taken by itself, needs one qualification: by arbitrary convention, science utilizes in the testing of hypotheses two principles, namely, "Occam's razor" (or the principle of parsimony) and the principle of fruitfulness, neither of which is dependent upon the relationship of signifying or pointing. Both of these principles serve to discriminate between hypotheses resting upon equally (that is to say, completely) valid grounding, so far as sheer *evidential* relationship is concerned. However, both are characteristic of the same pragmatic outlook which sanctions the kind of reliance upon reflection advocated in this study, so that the assertion in the text is warranted *within its present context*.

[69]Even the discovery by an alert youngster that most scholars fix the size of Alexander's army (at the Granicus) at 37,000 will not disturb him.

[70]Robinson, James Harvey, *The Humanizing of Knowledge*.

[71]"Findings of the National Survey of the Education of Teachers," *Twelfth Yearbook of the American Association of Teachers Colleges*, 1933, p. 116.

[72]Bagley, William C. and Alexander, Thomas: *The Teacher of the Social Studies*, p. 46.

BIBLIOGRAPHY

American Association of Teachers Colleges Twelfth Yearbook: *Findings of the National Survey of the Education of Teachers*, 1933.

American Historical Association, Commission on the Social Studies: *Conclusions and Recommendations*. New York: Charles Scribner's Sons, 1934.

Bagley, William C.: *The Teacher*. New York: Charles Scribner's Sons, 1937.

Bagley, William C., and Alexander, Thomas: *The Teacher of the Social Studies*. New York: Charles Scribner's Sons, 1937.

Balken, Eva Ruth: *Affective, Volitional, and Galvanic Factors in Learning*, Part of Ph.D. Thesis, Department of Psychology, 1930, The University of Chicago Libraries, Chicago. Reprinted from the Journal of Experimental Psychology, Vol. XVI, No. 1, February, 1933.

Barnes, Harry Elmer, ed.: *The History and Prospects of the Social Sciences*. New York: Knopf, 1925.

Beale, Howard K.: *Are American Teachers Free?* New York: Charles Scribner's Sons, 1936.

Beard, Charles A.: *A Charter for the Social Sciences*. New York: Charles Scribner's Sons, 1932.

Beard, Charles A.: "That Noble Dream". *American Historical*

Review, xli, October, 1935.

Beard, Charles A.: *The Nature of the Social Sciences*. New York: Charles Scribner's Sons, 1934.

Beard, Charles A.: *The Nature of the Social Sciences in Relation to Objectives of Instruction*. New York: Charles Scribner's Sons, 1934.

Beard, Charles; Robinson, James Harvey; and Smith, Donnal V.: *Our Own Age*. Boston: Ginn and Company, 1937.

Billings, Neal: *A Determination of Generalizations Basic to the Social Studies Curriculum*. Baltimore: Warwick and York, 1929.

Bining, A. C. and D. H.: *Teaching the Social Studies in Secondary Schools*. New York: The McGraw-Hill Book Company, Inc., revised edition, 1941.

Bining, Arthur C.; Mohr, Walter H.; and McFeely, Richard H.: *Organizing the Social Studies in Secondary Schools*. New York: The McGraw-Hill Book Company, Inc., 1941.

Bode, Boyd H.: *Democracy as a Way of Life*. New York: The Macmillan Company, 1935.

Bode, Boyd H.: *Modern Educational Theories*. New York: The Macmillan Company, 1927.

Bowman, Isaiah: *Geography in Relation to the Social Sciences*. New York: Charles Scribner's Sons, 1934.

Byron, R. M.: *Teaching of History in Junior and Senior High Schools*. Boston: Ginn and Company, 1925.

Commission on Secondary School Curriculum, Report of the Committee on the Function of Science in General Education: *Science in General Education, Suggestions for Science Teachers in Secondary Schools and in the Lower Division of Colleges*. New York: D. Appleton-Century Company, Inc., 1938.

Columbia Associates in Philosophy: *An Introduction to Reflective Thinking*. Boston: Houghton Mifflin Company, 1923.

Cook, Edgar Marion: *An Analysis of the Methods Used in Solving a Rational Learning Problem*. Nashville, Tennessee: George Peabody College for Teachers, 1936.

Cook, Lloyd Allen: "The Society in Which Children Live", *Twelfth Yearbook* (1941) of the National Council for the Social Studies.

Counts, George S.: *The Social Foundations of Education*. New York: Charles Scribner's Sons, 1934.

Craven, Avery: *Democracy in American Life, A Historical Review*. Chicago: The University of Chicago Press, 1941.

Curti, Margaret W.: *Child Psychology*. New York: Longmans, 1938.

Curti, Merle: *The Social Ideas of American Educators*. Charles Scribner's Sons, 1935.

Dawson, Edgar: *Teaching the Social Studies*. New York: The Macmillan Company, 1927.

Dennis, George: *Cities and Cemeteries of Etruria*, 2 Vol. London: Dutton and Company, revised edition, 1907.

Dewey, John: *Democracy and Education, An Introduction to the Philosophy of Education*. New York: The Macmillan Company, 1925.

Dewey, John: "Education for a Changing Social Order". Proceedings (1934) of the National Education Association.

Dewey, John: *How We Think*. Boston: D. C. Heath and Company, 1910.

Dewey, John: *Logic: The Theory of Inquiry*. New York: Henry Holt and Company, 1939.

Duvall, T. G.: *Great Thinkers*. London: Oxford University Press, 1937.

Educational Policies Commission: *The Unique Function of Education in American Democracy*. Washington: National Education Association, 1937.

Ellis, Edward Sylvester: *Young People's History of Our Country*. Boston, 1898.

Everett, Samuel and Others: *Challenge to Secondary Education*. 1935.

Fancler, D. G.; and Crawford, C. C.: *Teaching the Social Studies*. Los Angeles: C. C. Crawford, 1932.

Fay, Sidney Bradshaw: *The Origins of the World War*, Vol. II, *After Sarajevo: Immediate Causes of the War*. New York: The Macmillan Company, 1929.

Franz, Shepherd Ivory; Layman, John D.; Kilduff, Sybil; Morgan, Roy C.; Davis, Evalene F.; Eaton, Amerette G.; McCulloch, T. L.: *The Possibility of Space Perception by Tactile Means*. Berkeley, California: The University of California Press, 1933.

Fraser, Sir John: *The Golden Bough*. New York: The Macmillan Company, 1922.

Gollancz, Victor; and Somervell, David: *Political Education at a Public School*. London: W. Collins Sons and Company, Ltd., 1918.

Harrison, Frederic: *The Meaning of History*. New York: The Macmillan Company, 1894.

Horn, Ernest: *Methods of Instruction in the Social Studies*. New York: Charles Scribner's Sons, 1937.

Horn, Ernest: "Possible Defects in the Present Content of American History as Taught in the Schools". *Sixteenth Yearbook* (1917) of the National Society for the Study of Education. Part I, pp. 156–172.

James, William: *The Moral Equivalent of War*. New York: American Association for International Conciliation, 1910.

John Dewey Society Third Yearbook: *Democracy and the Curriculum*. New York: D. Appleton-Century Company, 1939.

Johnson, Henry: *An Introduction to the History of the Social Sciences in Schools*. New York: Charles Scribner's Sons, 1932.

Johnson, Henry: *Teaching of History in Elementary and Secondary Schools, with Applications to Allied Studies*. New York: The Macmillan Company, revised edition, 1940.

Kilpatrick, William Heard: *Foundations of Method: Informal Talks on Teaching*. New York: The Macmillan Company, 1925.

Kilpatrick, William Heard: *Remaking the Curriculum*. New York: Newson and Company, 1936.

Kirkland, Edward C.: *A History of American Economic Life*. New York: F. S. Crofts and Company, 1939.

Klapper, Paul: *The Teaching of History*. New York: D. Appleton and Company, 1926.

Knight, Edgar W.: *Education in the United States*. Boston: Ginn and Company, 1934.

Krey, A. C.: *A Regional Program for the Social Studies*. New York: The Macmillan Company, 1938.

Langer, William, ed.: *An Encyclopaedia of World History*. Boston: The Houghton Mifflin Company, 1940.

Langlois, Charles V.; and Seignobos, Charles: *Introduction to the Study of History*. Translated by G. G. Berry. London: Duckworth and Company, 1925.

Lynd, Robert S., and Helen M.: *Middletown*. New York: Harcourt Brace and Company, 1929.

McMurry, Charles A.: *Special Method in History, A Complete Outline of a Course of Study in History for the Grades Below the High School*. New York: The Macmillan Company, 1915.

Marshall, Leon C.; and Goetz, Rachel M.: *Curriculum Making in the Social Studies*. New York: Charles Scribner's Sons, 1938.

Marx, Karl: *Value, Price and Profit*. New York: International Publishers, 1935.

Marx, Karl: *Wage-labour and Capital*. New York: International Publishers, 1935.

Moulton, H. G.: *Income and Economic Progress*. Washington: Brookings Institution, 1935.

National Council for the Social Studies: *The Future of the Social Studies: Proposals for an Experimental Social Studies Curriculum*. James A. Michener, ed. Curriculum Series, No. 1. The Council, 1939.

National Education Association, Department of Superintendence: *Fourteenth Yearbook*. Washington: National Education Association, 1936.

Nevins, Allan: "American History for Americans", *New York Times Magazine*, May 3, 1942.

Nevins, Allan: *The Gateway to History*. Boston: D. C. Heath and Company, 1938.

Newman, H. H., ed.: *The Nature of the World and of Man*. Garden City, New York: Garden City Publishing Company, Inc., 1927.

Pierce, B. L.: *Civic Attitudes in American School Textbooks*. Chicago: The University of Chicago Press, 1930.

Pinkevitch, Albert P.: *The New Education in the Soviet Republic*. Translated by Nucia Perlmutter. New York: John Day and Company, 1929.

Rattner, Joseph: *John Dewey's Philosophy*. New York, 1940.

Robinson, James Harvey: *The Humanizing of Knowledge*. New York: The Macmillan Company, 1911.

Robinson, James Harvey: *The Mind in the Making, The Relation of Intelligence to Social Reform*. New York: Harpers and Brothers, 1921.

Robinson, James Harvey: *The New History*. New York: The Macmillan Company, 1912.

Rugg, Harold O.: *Content of American History as Taught in Seventh and Eighth Grades*. School of Education Bulletin, No. 16. Urbana, Illinois: The University of Illinois Press, 1915.

Russell, Bertrand: *An Inquiry Into Meaning and Truth*. New York: Norton and Company, 1940.

Seldes, George: *Freedom of the Press*. New York: Bobbs-Merrill Company, 1935.

Smith, Donnal V.: *Social Learning for Youth in the Secondary School*. New York: Charles Scribner's Sons, 1927.

Smith, Theodore Clarke: "Writing of American History in America, from 1884 to 1934". *American Historical Review*, xl, April, 1935.

Steffens, Lincoln: *The Autobiography of Lincoln Steffens*. New York: Harcourt Brace and Company, 1931.

Stormzand, Martin James: *American History Teaching and Testing*. New York: The Macmillan Company, 1927.

Stormzand, Martin James; and Lewis, R. H.: *New Methods in the Social Studies*. New York: Farrar and Rinehart, 1935.

Sumner, William Graham: *Folkways, A Study of the Sociological Importance of Usages, Manners, Customs, Mores, and Morals*. Boston: Ginn and Company, 1906.

Swindler, Robert E.: *Social Studies Instruction*. New York: Prentice Hall, 1933.

Tawney, R. H.: *The Acquisitive Society*. New York: Harcourt Brace and Company, 1920.

Trotter, William: *Instincts of the Herd in Peace and War*. New York: The Macmillan Company.

Tryon, Rolla M.: *The Teaching of History in Junior and Senior High Schools*. Boston: Ginn and Company, 1921.

Warren, Charles: *Odd Byways in American History*. Cambridge: Harvard University Press, 1942.

Washburne, Carleton W.: "Building a Fact Course in History and Geography". *Twenty-Second Yearbook* (1923). The National Society for the Study of Education, Part II, pp. 99–111.

Wayland, John W.: *How to Teach American History, A Handbook for Teachers and Students*. New York: The Macmillan Company, 1923.

Wesley, Edgar Bruce: *Teaching the Social Studies*. Boston: D. C. Heath and Company, 1942.

Woodworth, Robert S.: *Experimental Psychology*. New York: Henry Holt and Company, 1938.

Woodworth, Robert S.: *Psychology, A Study of Mental Life*. New York: Henry Holt and Company, 1921.

Index